Metroplex Monsters

Metroplex Monsters

DALLAS DEMONS, FORT WORTH GOATMEN & OTHER TERRORS OF THE TRINITY RIVER

Jason McLean

Published by The History Press
Charleston, SC
www.historypress.com

Copyright © 2020 by Jason McLean
All rights reserved

First published 2020

Manufactured in the United States

ISBN 9781467145435

Library of Congress Control Number: 2020940194

Notice: The information in this book is true and complete to the best of our knowledge. It is offered without guarantee on the part of the author or The History Press. The author and The History Press disclaim all liability in connection with the use of this book.

All rights reserved. No part of this book may be reproduced or transmitted in any form whatsoever without prior written permission from the publisher except in the case of brief quotations embodied in critical articles and reviews.

Contents

Introduction	7
Davy Crockett's Creature: A Brief History of Bigfoot in Texas	11
What Is Texas Bigfoot?: Sasquatch or Shaman	15
The Green Wall	20
Fort Worth Freaks	26
The Evolution of the Goatman	31
Dallas Demons	46
The Goatman Goes Traveling	55
The Goatmen throughout History	59
La Mujer Lechuza, Also Known as the Lechuza of Oak Cliff	62
Bridges and Paranormal Entities	69
Mountain Creek Monster: Bigfoot of Grand Prairie and the Best Southwest Cities	74
The Ten Mile Creek: DeSoto	92
Dragons through History	99
Aquatic Anomalies	107
Conclusion	123
Bibliography	125
About the Author	128

Introduction

When people think of monsters like Bigfoot or the Loch Ness Monster, creatures that seemingly belong to another time or world, the Dallas/Fort Worth Metroplex certainly doesn't come to mind as a popular stomping ground for these particularly peculiar abnormalities. I know it's easy to assume that cryptozoological creatures (animals undiscovered by modern science but known in folklore and mythology) could only exist in far-off locales like the bottom of the ocean or impenetrable forests—if they exist at all. Like most people, I assumed that nothing (certainly nothing as large as Sasquatch) could escape detection in a modern metropolis, but I have learned that this assumption is wrong.

Now, to be fair, the idea of these anomalous and undiscovered creatures lurking among the shadows of the seventh largest metroplex region in the country does seem preposterous at first (or even second) glance. After all, the Dallas/Fort Worth conurbation is home to 7.8 million residents, the F-22 Raptor is assembled in Fort Worth, Dallas is home to numerous Fortune 500 companies and D/FW Airport (officially Dallas/Fort Worth International Airport) services almost 33 million passengers annually, making it the fourth busiest airport in the United States. It seems impossible to hide giant bipedal apes and prehistoric creatures next to a Six Flags theme park or a GM assembly plant, but despite the omnipresent concrete of urban sprawl, stories of strange and undiscovered beings do haunt the metroplex. Some are urban legends, evidence of a culture evolving from an agricultural base into an industrialized powerhouse, while others

INTRODUCTION

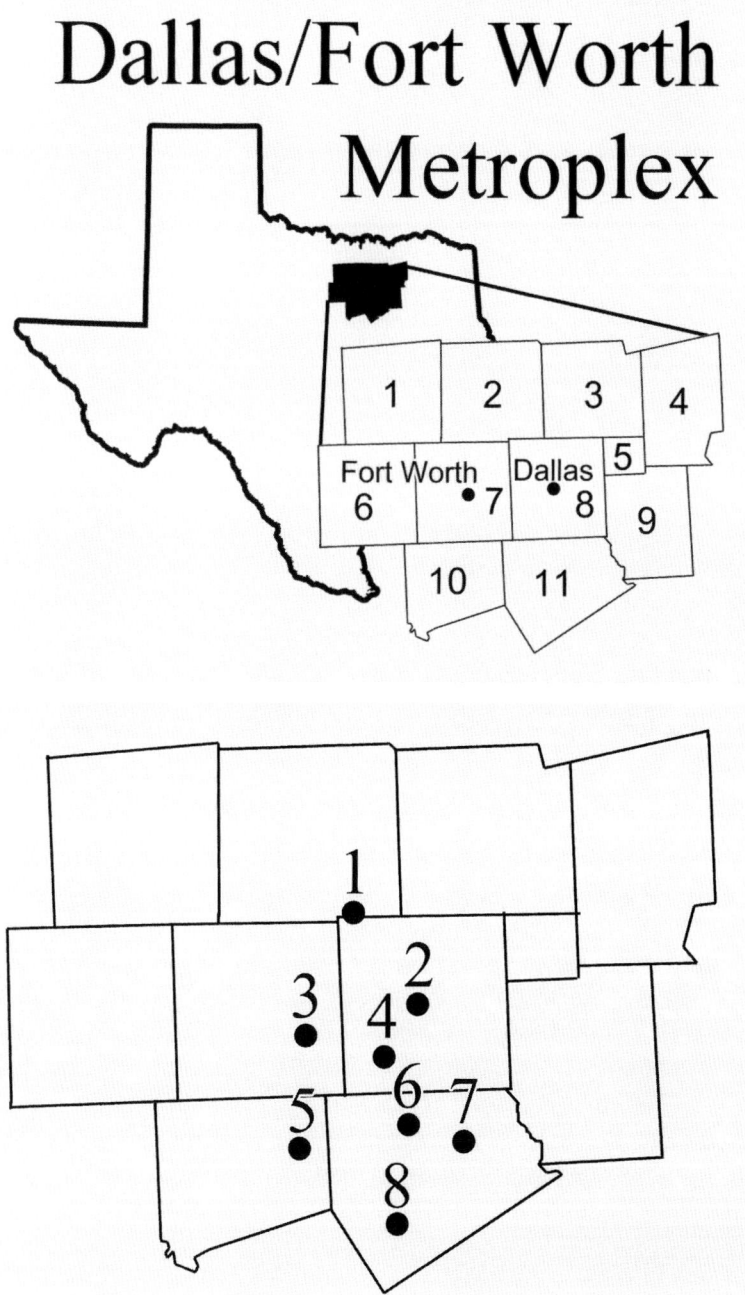

Introduction

appear to be living relics of an ancient world that go about their lives happily ignoring us, only being seen because the region's constant growth forces us to continue to encroach on their habitat. But there are some creatures that seem to be somewhere in between—predatory phantoms brought with us from disparate cultures throughout history that reach out to specific victims, inflicting terror and confusion.

OPPOSITE, TOP
1) Wise County 2) Denton County 3) Collin County 4) Hunt County 5) Rockwall County 6) Parker County 7) Tarrant County 8) Dallas County 9) Kaufman County 10) Johnson County 11) Ellis County.

OPPOSITE, BOTTOM
1) Denton 2) Dallas 3) Fort Worth 4) Mountain Creek Area (Grand Prairie, Duncanville, Cedar Hill Border) 5) Cleburne 6) Waxahachie 7) Ennis 8) Italy.

Davy Crockett's Creature

A Brief History of Bigfoot in Texas

If you're like me, you'd expect that if something like Bigfoot existed in Texas, then it must have lived here for a very long time, which would mean we should have long histories of contacts and ancient mythologies surrounding these beings—not just a few newspaper clippings about a bunch of scared teens from the late 1960s. But the truth is that Bigfoot is and has always been the eight-hundred-pound gorilla of Texas mythology (yes, I stand by that pun); in fact, the most famous (if not controversial) historical Texas Sasquatch sighting occurred in 1836 with famed hero of the Alamo Congressman David Crockett himself. The account comes from a letter Mr. Crockett wrote to his brother-in-law Abner Burgin while the King of the Wild Frontier was exploring the woods around Nacogdoches, Texas (about 180 miles southeast of Dallas):

> *William and I were pushing through some thicket, clearing the way, when I sat down to mop my brow. I sat for a spell, watching as William made his good and fine progress. I removed my boots and sat with my rations, thinking the afternoon a fine time to lunch. As the birds whistled and chirped and I ate my small and meager ration, I tapped my axe upon the opposite end of the felled tree, I rested upon.*
>
> *Whether it was the axe's disturbance or possibly the heat of the high sun which caused an apparition to slowly form in front of my eyes, I know not. As a Christian man, I swear to you, Abe, that what spirit came upon me was the shape and shade of a large ape man, the likes we might expect*

Metroplex Monsters

Depiction of the monster encountered by Davy Crockett. *Illustration by the author.*

among the more bellicose and hostile Indian tribes of the Territories. The shade formed into the most deformed and ugly countenance. Covered in wild hair, with small and needling eyes, large broken rows of teeth, and the height of three foundlings [just over eight feet tall], I spit upon the ground the bread I was eating.

The Monster then addressed a warning to me. Abner, it told me to return from Texas, to flee this Fort and to abandon this lost cause. When I began to question this, the Creature spread upon the wind like the morning steam swirls off a frog pond. I swear to you, Abner, that whatever meat or sausage disagreed with me that afternoon, I forswore all beef and hog for a day or so afterward.

The congressman's encounter is extremely controversial in the world of Bigfoot research because of Crockett's description of the thing's phantom-like qualities and ability to speak, but Mr. Crockett was known for his flamboyance and hyperbole in speech and writing. So, it's not necessary for us to take his account of it appearing and disappearing as literal but instead as a well-crafted story of this creature coming into his view and then quickly blending into the foliage—an attribute many people describe to this day as "disappearing." As for this tall terror speaking, many people who stumble into a Bigfoot's territory (often thought to be where the family group has nested for the day) have an extreme feeling of fear and that they need to leave the area immediately. It may be that Crockett's interpretation of the encounter and these same emotions were taken as a message that we see as prophetic in retrospect.

Whatever the answer for this strange encounter might be, I'd like to point out that the famed frontiersman was in the perfect location for a Bigfoot sighting. Even to this day, the region of the Piney Woods (a coniferous forest region of East Texas that continues into southeastern Oklahoma, Louisiana and Arkansas) that Crockett was exploring has the highest number of Bigfoot sightings in Texas. It is also important to note that this area was home to the Caddo, a American Indian tribe that was indigenous to the Louisiana/East Texas region and had established successful satellite villages as far west as the Grand Prairie/Arlington area strewn along the Trinity River and its tributaries. In fact, one of the largest of these expansionist locations was in the Mountain Creek area of Dallas County, where Joe Pool Lake is now. The Caddo often warned visitors of a strange and standoffish tribe of giants, called the Stick Indians, who were one with nature. Many researchers believe that the Stick Indians were actually Bigfoot family groups and that they were given their name because of how Sasquatch marked their territory. Though somewhat controversial, many researchers believe that Bigfoot will denote areas they inhabit by bending young saplings together in X formations or even breaking trees at about six to seven feet high. For the Caddo, the Stick Indians (a name also used by several other tribes across the United States) were a secretive tribe to be respected, if not slightly feared.

Another famous event often attributed to a Sasquatch occurred the year following Congressman Crockett's sighting in 1837, when enslaved people working in the Navidad River bottoms, near what is now Sublime, Texas (about 240 miles south of Dallas), started telling stories of the "thing that comes in the night" or just the "thing." For thirteen years, the Wild Man of the Navidad, as he is now known to researchers, stole food and domesticated pigs in the night, only to disappear into the woods around the encampments. There are competing claims that the Wild Man was captured around 1850, though it turned out to be a runaway slave who was later resold into bondage. While a runaway slave may have been captured in this area, many researchers question these accounts as an explanation for the Wild Man phenomenon.

Even ignoring the descriptions of the Wild Man being covered in coarse brown hair, it is the mysterious monster's odd behavior—like not stealing money or other items of monetary value and borrowing tools in the night and later returning them cleaned and polished—that leads many to question the runaway slave theory. Such behavior appears inconsistent with the actions of a person on the run. One account tries to explain this away, stating that the man was an African prince who didn't speak the languages of the enslaved people or the enslavers (Spanish and English). But that still doesn't explain why he wouldn't have just stolen the tools and resources he needed to survive in the woods, where he would have been removed from the threat of recapture.

In the 1870s, there were accounts of a large humanoid creature named the Monster that would let out a mournful and terrifying cry while traversing the creeks near Ensign, Texas (about thirty-five miles south of Dallas), in Ellis County. Now defunct and replaced by the larger city of Ennis, the settlement of Ensign was located between Chambers Creek, Cummins Creek and Waxahachie Creek near where Bardwell Lake is now. The Monster was also recorded in Waxahachie Creek near Reagor Springs (eight miles west of Ennis) in the 1920s and in Red Oak Creek near Rocket (about twenty miles south of Dallas and fifteen miles northwest of Ennis) in the 1930s. But the tales of the Monster or the Creature and even the Hinkey Man of Ten Mile Creek (found in Lancaster and DeSoto, north of Red Oak) would all be (in the D/FW Metroplex anyway) replaced by the goatman in 1969, with the infamous Lake Worth Monster encounters.

Fun fact: The 160,000-plus acres that make up the Davy Crockett National Forest were named for the famed pioneer and hero of the Alamo because of his exploration of the region.

What Is Texas Bigfoot?

Sasquatch or Shaman

Before we discuss D/FW's most famous cryptid, or how these furry folklore figures can remain hidden in our modern world, I want to address a common theme that might have stood out in many of the early Bigfoot accounts and how it lines up with a modern theory that we need to explore. This is the feral human or shaman theory. A brief summation of the theory goes like this: all Bigfoot sightings aren't an unknown species of giant ape or human cousin but rather are American Indian shamans on spirit journeys or are feral humans. For some American Indian tribes, there are traditions of medicine men going on prolonged sojourns in which tools are left behind to "learn the ways of the earth" and bring those revelations back to the tribe. It is claimed that this process, for certain tribes, can make those undergoing it appear more like an animal than a human, as the shaman's hair becomes unruly, and they will adorn themselves with fur. A feral human (someone who has eschewed civilization for personal, religious or mental health issues) will become similarly disheveled and unkempt.

The theory is appealing for several reasons. First, it does explain why it is so hard to find Bigfoot in the wild, as they are only "in the wild" for a short time during a vision quest and are living normal human lives the rest of the time. Second, Bigfoot as a misidentified human in animal skins explains why, so often, DNA tests on purported Bigfoot evidence often return as bear or human instead of as an unknown primate or genetically divergent human relative (Neanderthal or Denisovan). Third, it conveniently solves the issue of Davy Crockett's letter and other reported encounters where language was heard. If the creature/Bigfoot Crockett saw was an American Indian spiritual leader on a vision quest, then the idea of him receiving a verbal warning to leave Texas, to "flee this Fort and to abandon this lost cause," isn't so hard to believe. Crockett himself even noted in his letter that the creature might be found among the more "bellicose and hostile Indian tribes of the Territories," indicating that he didn't see this monster as entirely nonhuman. This would mean that the message Crockett received was a prophetic message from a vision the shaman had. Or it could have been an attempt to scare the European settlers out of the area and only appears prophetic in retrospect.

Often used as evidence to bolster this theory was a purported Bigfoot sighting that many claim was a misidentified shaman. In the late summer of 2017, a self-described shaman named Gawain MacGregor was allegedly observed on a vision quest in South Carolina and was mistaken for Bigfoot by John Bruner and a group of local cryptozoologists whom Mr. Bruner was leading on an expedition. (A cryptozoologist is someone who researches and seeks out evidence for the existence of scientifically undiscovered creatures that are recorded in folklore and mythology. These creatures are called "cryptids," and the term was coined by Bernard Heuvelmans and Ivan T. Sanderson.) Mr. MacGregor was wearing an "animal suit" of squirrel skins, which included a mask that covered his face entirely and did have a Bigfoot look to it (the conical head and pronounced brow ridge). While I agree that cases of wild men or feral humans (due to choice, religious practice or mental illness) have occurred throughout history, still occur today and almost certainly play a role in broader Bigfoot lore, I think that this particular event actually exposes why the shaman/feral human theory is not a credible explanation for the Bigfoot phenomenon.

First, on a practical level, Bigfoot sightings occur (forget the worldwide encounters) all over Texas. There are literally dozens (probably hundreds, if truth be told) of recorded sightings from every corner of this great state. How many shamans would it take to account for all of them? Let's ignore all of the stories going back centuries or even decades. How many actual American Indian medicine men and New Age shamans going on vision quests in animal costumes (actively trying to avoid human contact) would it take to accommodate all of the sightings in Texas over the last ten years alone? Dozens? Hundreds? Second, Mr. MacGregor's suit looks like a man in a suit with a very large mask. It is important to note that John Bruner, who (at the time of the event) ran the Facebook group Bigfoot

Rendering of an American Indian shaman (*left*), the Sasquatch observed by Jeff Stewart (*center*) and Gawain MacGregor in his shaman costume (*right*). *Illustration by the author.*

911 and whose sighting in the Pisgah National Park occurred with eight other members from that group, denied seeing MacGregor. In an article published by the BBC on August 10, 2017, Mr. Bruner claimed that after looking at images of Mr. MacGregor's costume, it was his opinion that the self-proclaimed shaman was not what he and other witnesses observed.

However, even if we assume that Mr. MacGregor's suit could miraculously trick someone at a distance, it certainly could not deceive anyone within one hundred feet of the ritualized apparel, which brings me to Jeff Stewart's encounters.

Mr. Stewart had two notable encounters on his family's property in Panola County (about 130 miles east of Dallas), which is bordered by the Sabine River. Given that his first encounter happened at night when he was an adolescent, I think that his second meeting will be more advantageous for our purposes. You see, Mr. Stewart is not just someone who is familiar with the East Texas woods as a native to the region, but he is also a professional outdoorsman whose expertise on the wilds of the region is recognized by several naturalist and outdoor enthusiast magazines. This is important because on one late spring/early summer day in 2017, Jeff came face-to-face with another Sasquatch. He was out collecting mayhaw berries (a tart fruit indigenous to swampy areas of the southern United States that is often jellied) when he heard the rustling of tree branches above him and then the crashing impact of a heavy figure landing on the ground less than thirty feet behind him. He reported:

> *Obviously, between that night encounter and a few other things that happened, I knew they were on the property, so I didn't freak out when I saw him. I didn't reach for my gun because I didn't want to scare him or make him feel threatened. I figured he was waiting in the trees for a wild hog to come by as I was near a hog trail, which is why I was armed. I guess he figured I scared off any chance of lunch and wanted me to leave. He looked like a person with a really broad, flat nose, but he was covered in hair. It wasn't too thick—I could see the skin and muscles underneath, and he was ripped. At first, he was crouched down like Spider-Man, but his back was straight up, and his arms were still so long that his palms were flat on the ground. Then he stood up and walked off, and I got out of there. He stood like six and a half feet high.*

When I asked Jeff if this could have been someone in a costume, his reply was an emphatic "No. No way this was a normal guy. His arms were way too long to be like you or me, plus he was less than thirty feet from me in broad daylight. Whatever he was, he wasn't in a costume. This was something entirely different." Though smaller than the Sasquatch normally reported around the D/FW Metroplex (Mr. Stewart probably came across a younger male closer to the nesting site), it was clear that what he saw was not human—or at least human as we know it. This was not a shaman on a vision quest or a person who had rejected civilized life, but a creature not known to science.

So, if not feral humans or American Indian medicine men on ritualistic walkabouts, what are these creatures? Well, thus far no one really knows. It is clear from the accounts collected that something haunts the creeks and rivers of Texas—something smart, large and secretive; but "something" is the best word we have. For some notable researchers, Sasquatch is a relic population of bipedal apes, like *Gigantopithecus*, which is believed to have been an eight- to ten-foot-tall relative of the orangutan. Other researchers see Sasquatch as a missing link, something that links humans to apes. But perhaps the answer is more complicated and nuanced than first assumed. What if the answer is that everyone is correct?

Archaeology proves that at one time our planet had several subspecies of humans all living together at the same time: the *Denisova hominins*, *Homo neanderthalensis* and *Homo floresiensis* (lovingly nicknamed the hobbit people). Recent genetic analysis has even indicated the possibility of a few more genetically distinct hominid species that all lived contemporary with modern *Homo sapiens*. We fought, traded and interbred with these different humans, according to DNA, so what if that never really changed? What if Sasquatch is a relic population of one of these other human subspecies that long ago rejected civilization for a way of life that kept them one with nature and chooses to keep itself separated from us to avoid our culture polluting them?

Some researchers reject this out of hand, given how significantly different from us Sasquatch appears. However, I would point out that an eight-foot-tall hairy human can still be a human in the same way that an Irish wolfhound that, while standing on its hind legs, can look down on a full-grown man is the same species as the teacup chihuahua that fits in a socialite's purse. A giant, hirsute human is still a human—just a different kind of human. That being said, all we have is theory, for now at least. As of the writing of this book, the only thing we know for sure about Davy Crockett's monster or the Caddo's Stick Indians or our modern Bigfoot is that we just do not know what they are. We only know that people have seen them for as long as we have been here, and people still see them to this day.

The Green Wall

Like most people, I always assumed that if the wild and secretive man-beast we call Sasquatch existed, he would be wandering the untamed wilderness of the Pacific Northwest or some exotic locale shrouded in mystery—not in the yard of a middle-class suburban family in Texas's D/FW Metroplex. Even those researchers who note how "Squatchy" deep East Texas is because of its vast forests and swamps have trouble with Bigfoot sightings in and around Dallas/Fort Worth due to the perceived lack of green spaces in the Metroplex area.

While we have moved past people envisioning D/FW existing in an arid desert surrounded by oil wells and littered with tumbleweeds, Dallas certainly isn't known for its dense and impenetrable forests or swamps. One of the reasons cattle and cotton became the main agricultural exports for the region is that it sits on a fairly solid limestone bedrock, which makes the soil very shallow. This means that even though North Texas has an average rainfall sufficient for larger tree species, the shallow soil prevents those that can survive from taking root or rooting far enough down to grow larger than ten or twenty feet high. This results in large areas of wild grasses and a smattering of smaller scrub trees, like cedar and mesquite, which makes clearing trees for crops a simple matter.

In fact, the area is so well suited for cotton that in the 1920s, Ellis County (just south of Dallas and home to the aforementioned towns of Reagor Springs, Waxahachie and Ensgin) was the top cotton-producing county in the world, and despite the area's industrialization, it remains an important

Field south of Highway 287, just west of 67. *Courtesy of author.*

cash crop to this day. All of this is to say that even for those living in D/FW, the metroplex would seem a less-than-ideal location for hiding eight-foot-tall bipedal apes. But there is one place in D/FW where the dense foliage can be described as "impenetrable" and is deceptively massive—even to those native to the area.

From use as navigable trade routes to irrigation and water sources, the Trinity and Brazos Rivers, with their associated tributaries, have made life possible in Dallas for centuries. Due to yearly flooding, the areas around these waterways have significantly deeper soil, allowing for forests full of much larger trees and much denser foliage. OK, perhaps "forest" is too ambitious of a description, so we'll call them "green spaces," but they do exist.

These green spaces hug the rivers and creeks of North Texas and are full of trees like oak, pecan and bois d'arc (pronounced "bodark" and also known as the Osage orange). Due to the deeper soil and access to more water, many of these trees can reach fifty, seventy or even one hundred feet tall, making them titans when compared to their diminutive neighbors. Moreover, the aforementioned yearly flooding means that areas around the waterways, even though they cut through many of the most populous cities and towns that compose the metroplex, are often entirely given over to the trees. Combine this with conservancy efforts that create state-protected preserves that limit human activity, and you have an entire network of connected wooded areas that are largely uninterrupted and (somewhat) undisturbed. Interestingly, on the outer edges of these heavily wooded green spaces, because the trees can't grow large enough or densely enough

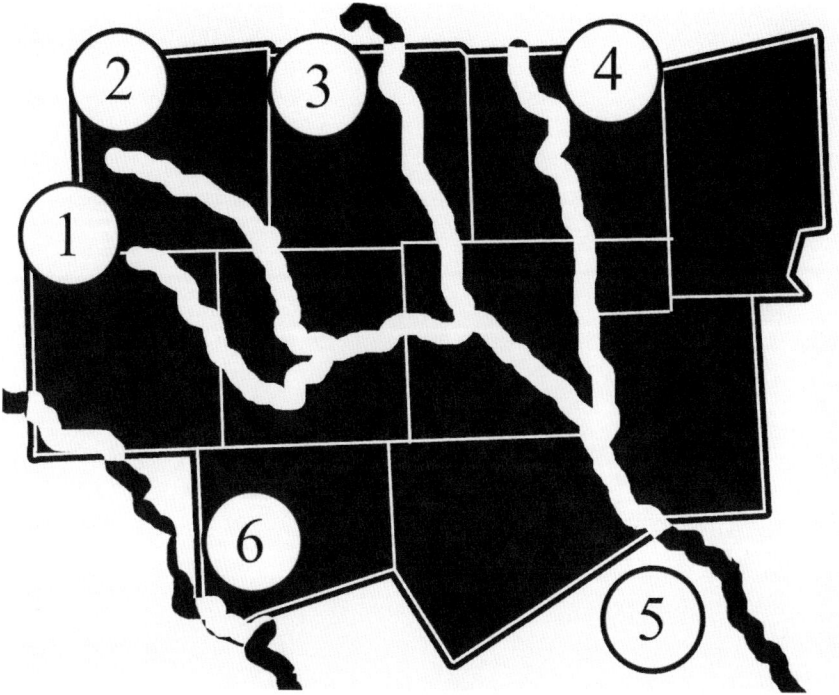

Map of the Trinity and Brazos Rivers. 1) West Fork of the Trinity River 2) Clear Fork of the Trinity River 3) Elm Fork of the Trinity River 4) East Fork of the Trinity River 5) Trinity River 6) Brazos.

to prevent smaller flora like grass or shrubbery from growing, an extremely thick layer of small- and medium-size plant life thrives. The result of this is a "green wall" that separates human civilization from a wild and difficultly navigated green space full of untamed nature.

A perfect example of how dense this green wall is can be found along Interstate 20 in Grand Prairie, where it crosses over the Fish Creek Preserve.

As you can see in the photographs, visibility from the road and surrounding parking lots is at best three or four feet, assuming there is any visibility at all. This is why, despite being flanked by two movie theaters, dozens of restaurants and warehouses, numerous residential areas and one of Texas's largest, most traveled highways, the Fish Creek Preserve is home to several recent Bigfoot sightings we address later in this book.

If the idea of a green wall hiding undiscovered creatures in plain sight seems farfetched, it should be noted that the city of Irving has a serious feral hog problem. For those unfamiliar with the area, Irving is located just east of Dallas and is basically a continuation of Dallas's urbanization.

Seventy-five-foot-high oak tree located along the Waxahachie Creek on westbound Highway 287 in Midlothian, Texas. *Courtesy of author.*

Home to Frito-Lay, as well as many other large manufacturers, the city is heavily industrialized and is also home to hundreds of feral hogs that most inhabitants never see. Despite trapping efforts in Irving and other surrounding Dallas suburbs, according to a 2017 article by Mary Mapes (published in *D Magazine*), the number of feral hogs in Dallas County could run in the thousands.

Fish Creek Preserve in Grand Prairie, Texas. The top photo is from within the creek and the photo below is less than one hundred feet away, from the street side of the same tree line. *Courtesy of author.*

This odd collection of flat grasslands and dense, contiguous greenspaces makes the cities and suburbs of the D/FW region like concrete islands with the wild and untamed areas protected by a green wall that encompasses the waterways. But perhaps the most important images come from the city of Dallas's southern border with the suburb of Hutchins, where I-20 crosses the Trinity. It's close enough for the skyline of downtown Dallas

Trinity River bottoms, Dallas, Texas. *Courtesy of author.*

to be observed from this bridge, but to look at the Trinity River bottoms, you'd think you were in the middle of nowhere, miles from civilization in an untamed wilderness.

There have been numerous accounts of Bigfoot sightings and encounters coming out of this area, and it is in this swath of wilderness that the creatures that haunt the D/FW Metroplex hide. These amazing animals (perhaps humans according to some) are protected from civilization's intrusion behind the green wall that we deliberately preserve and often strengthen. This meandering barrier along the banks and bottoms of the Trinity River and its tributaries is what allows them to live their separate lives, completely hidden from our gaze—at least until one of us crosses that border and it makes the news.

Fort Worth Freaks

Lovingly dubbed "Cowtown" due to its importance as a stop along the legendary cattle drive known as the Chisholm Trail, Fort Worth started off as a military fort located on a bluff at the mouth of the Trinity River's Clear Fork. Millions of heads of cattle were driven up the trail through Fort Worth for years until the Texas and Pacific (T&P) Railway was completed in 1876. The railway transformed Fort Worth from a mere rest stop into the Queen City of the Prairies by making the stockyards the epicenter for wholesale cattle trade in the West. This position of importance was cemented when Armour and Swift, two of the largest meatpacking companies in the country at the time, moved into the stockyards. Fort Worth became known as the Paris of the Plains due to the city's importance as a last stop to gather supplies and rest on the Chisholm Trail, and the arrival of the railroad only increased its popularity.

That being said, it should be noted that the Paris of the Plains had a dark side that was as wild and violent as anything seen in a John Wayne movie. The Bloody Third Ward, also known as Hell's Half Acre, was a block on the south side of the city full of saloons, gambling parlors and houses of ill repute. Hell's Half Acre was where the Fort Worth Water Gardens and Convention Center are now and was so violent that Timothy Isaiah Courtright, also known as Longhair Jim Courtright, was elected to tame the area and calm down the situation in 1876. By 1879, though his efforts effectively cut Fort Worth's murder rate by half, it was decided that his services in this particular position were no longer required when several legitimate businessmen noticed that it adversely affected their profitability.

Longhair Jim had a questionable history that would catch up with him in 1887 while trying to extort protection money from Luke Short, a gambler and gunfighter who owned a saloon and gambling hall named the White Elephant. Courtright had been drinking and called out Mr. Short, who eventually ended up killing the former lawman on Fort Worth's Main Street in a duel that went down like something from your favorite Western film. The event was witnessed and then immortalized by Luke Short's friend Bat Masterson in his book *Luke Short: A Dandy Gunfighter*. In his account of the duel, he said, "No time was wasted in the exchange of words once the men faced each other. Both drew their pistols at the same time, but, as usual, Short's spoke first and a bullet from a Colt's .45-calibre pistol went crashing through Courtright's body. The shock caused him to reel backward; then he got another and still another, and by the time his lifeless form had reached the floor, Luke had succeeded in shooting him five times."

But Bat Masterson and Luke Short weren't the only famous gamblers and gunfighters to frequent the Queen of the Prairies, as Doc Holliday and the Earp brothers would often come to town on the Gambler's Circuit. In fact, James Earp (the oldest brother) lived in Fort Worth during this infamous period. But by the early 1900s, reforms and progress eventually tamed the Acre, and Fort Worth prepared for the new century to come. It bears noting that in less than fifty years, Fort Worth had grown from a minor military post into a major agricultural capital that would be in a position to explode into a major economic powerhouse during World War II.

In 1917, General Motors opened its first manufacturing plant on West Seventh Street, near where Trinity Park is now, to build Chevrolet Series 490 automobiles. In that same year, the U.S. Army set up Camp Bowie just outside of Fort Worth. The success of the plant and training base meant that once World War I had ended, Fort Worth was able to expand and bring in larger industrial manufacturing and processing companies. This expansion put the city in a position to petition the military to construct its new heavy bomber factories in the area. The city eventually won. With the onset of World War II, not only would the heavy bomber manufacturing factories be set up in Fort Worth, but Texas as a whole would also become extremely important to the war effort.

Mild winters, fewer days of rain and abundant resources made Texas a major center for training and manufacturing, and most of Texas's industrial factories were centered in Houston and the D/FW Metroplex.

This meant that pilots who were being trained to drop bombs at the Five Points Field in Arlington, Texas (between Dallas and Fort Worth), were flying B-24 Liberators built at the heavy bomber factories run by Fleet and Consolidated Aircraft out of Fort Worth. Now known as the United States Air Force Plant 4 (owned by the U.S. Air Force but run by Lockheed Martin Aeronautics), this is home to the F-16 Fighting Falcon, F-22 Raptor and F-35 Lightning II.

Fun fact (sort of): The area that used to be Five Points Field, off Matlock Road and north of U.S. 287, still has subsurface unexploded training ordnance that was never recovered. Most of these bombs were the size of footballs and possess only enough black powder to fill a twelve-gauge shotgun shell so that the smoke could be seen from the plane.

As Fort Worth expanded post–World War II, it also benefitted from the growth of neighboring city Arlington (still in Tarrant County, for which Fort Worth is the county seat), where GM would open a new, much larger factory in 1954. It would eventually become home to the Texas Rangers, the Six Flags over Texas theme park and the Dallas Cowboys. Despite Fort Worth's rapid growth, becoming home to the construction of advanced military aircraft and the location for the second of two U.S. Bureau of Engraving and Printing mints, it has fully embraced and protected its history as the city Where the West Begins and its role in the mythos of the Wild West.

But I should mention that Fort Worth is famous for one other thing.

The Lake Worth Monster, also Known as the Greer Island Goatman

For nearly two months, the Fort Worth Police Department had been writing off calls they were receiving about a "monster" seen around Lake Worth's Greer Island as hoaxes or prank calls. All of that would change around midnight on July 10, 1969, when John Reichart, his wife and four friends encountered the goatman. The three couples had gathered near Greer Island when a large creature appeared. According to Jim Marrs of the *Fort Worth Star Telegram*, Mr. Reichart described it as being covered in scales and hair and "part man and part goat."

As preposterous as this description sounds, Mr. Marrs recorded patrolman James S. McGee as stating that he believed that the Reicharts were telling

Dallas Demons, Fort Worth Goatmen & Other Terrors of the Trinity River

Greer Island, Fort Worth Nature Center and Refuge. *Courtesy of author.*

the truth of their encounter, noting the genuine sense of fear the group clearly felt and the odd scrape that ran eighteen inches down Mr. Reichart's car. However, patrolman McGee also believed they were the victims of a prank—one that could become dangerous. Dangerous it would become—but not for the reason the patrolman believed.

Around midnight the following day, between twenty and forty people, including several police officers, gathered in the area to investigate the claims heard on a local radio station. Many had plans to perhaps physically subdue and capture the furry fiend and determine the truth of the matter (whether he was creature or prankster), but those went completely out the window when confronted with the creature. On hearing what Jack E. Harris described as a "pitiful cry" (as reported by Jim Marrs in an article published in the July 11 afternoon edition of the *Fort Worth Star Telegram*), the group recoiled in terror as the creature leapt from a bluff, grabbed a discarded spare tire—full sized with rim—and hurled it five hundred feet at the spectators.

The creature then rushed the terrified mob, causing the group to scatter in panic. "Those sheriff's men weren't any braver than we were," Mr. Harris recalled. "They ran to get in their car." The creature was universally described as a tall, hairy humanoid with light-colored fur.

Jim Stephens claimed that the creature was over seven feet tall, as it was substantially taller than he was (six feet four inches), and he provided an interesting description of the monster's appearance to local historian Sallie Ann Clarke, author of *The Lake Worth Monster*. "It was real big and human like with burnt scars all over its face, arms and chest," he said. Given that the creature jumped onto the hood of his Mustang and was only shaken off when he backed into a tree, the young Mr. Stephens had an excellent opportunity to look at it, and his observations are telling.

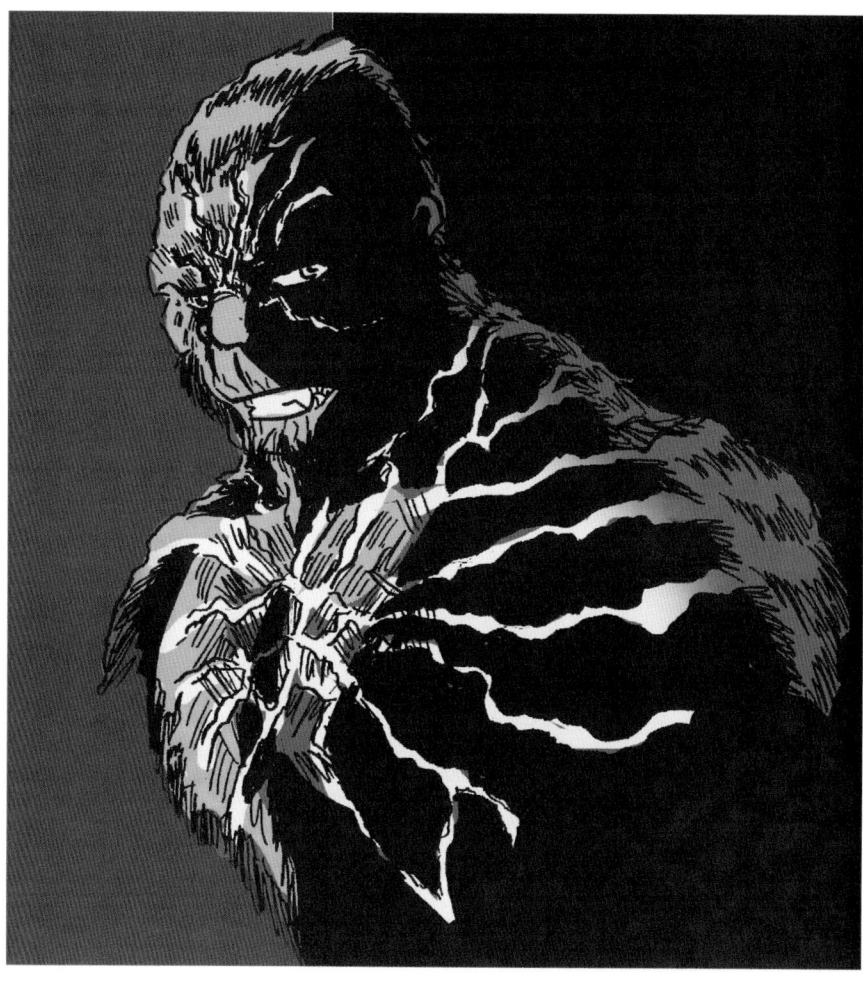

Drawing of the monster that John Reichart and Jim Stephens encountered. An explanation for the scales or burns over the face and upper body that were observed and mentioned by both Mr. Reichart and Mr. Stephens could be simple mange. Researcher and animal rescuer Jeff Stewart notes that dogs or feral animals suffering from the illness are often described as having scales or burn marks by people unfamiliar with the condition. *Illustration by the author.*

Researcher, wilderness expert and animal rescuer Jeff Stewart confirmed in an interview that animals suffering from mange can often be mistaken for burn victims or appear scaly to those unfamiliar with this disease. This might provide an explanation for the scales initially noted by Mr. Reichart.

The Evolution of the Goatman

The Greer Island Goatman Goes Gallivanting and Rewrites Metroplex Mythology

By the end of July 1969, the Sasquatch known as the Lake Worth Monster (or the Greer Island Goatman) was famous nationwide. For a brief moment, stories of a giant wild man with red glowing eyes and a penchant for throwing things at paparazzi filled news broadcasts and articles. Then, just as quickly as this kerfuffle began, the hirsute horror disappeared into the woods surrounding Lake Worth. But it wasn't too long before people around the D/FW Metroplex began seeing him everywhere. Perhaps the most well documented of these sightings occurred later that same year in the small town of Cedar Hill.

According to local historian Shirley Switzer Hendricks, Cedar Hill's goatman may have been the same seen at Lake Worth. She notes in the *History of Cedar Hill, Texas* that Mount Lebanon's goatman was first observed by firefighter Bobby Grashel during a nighttime rattlesnake hunt. Bobby had been hunting in the area around Pleasant Valley Cemetery when his flashlight hit a creature that he said resembled Lake Worth's Greer Island goatman. The local community had little reason to doubt Mr. Grashel's account, as he was an honest man of good standing in the community, but his claim was bolstered by the Halls family, who saw the same creature.

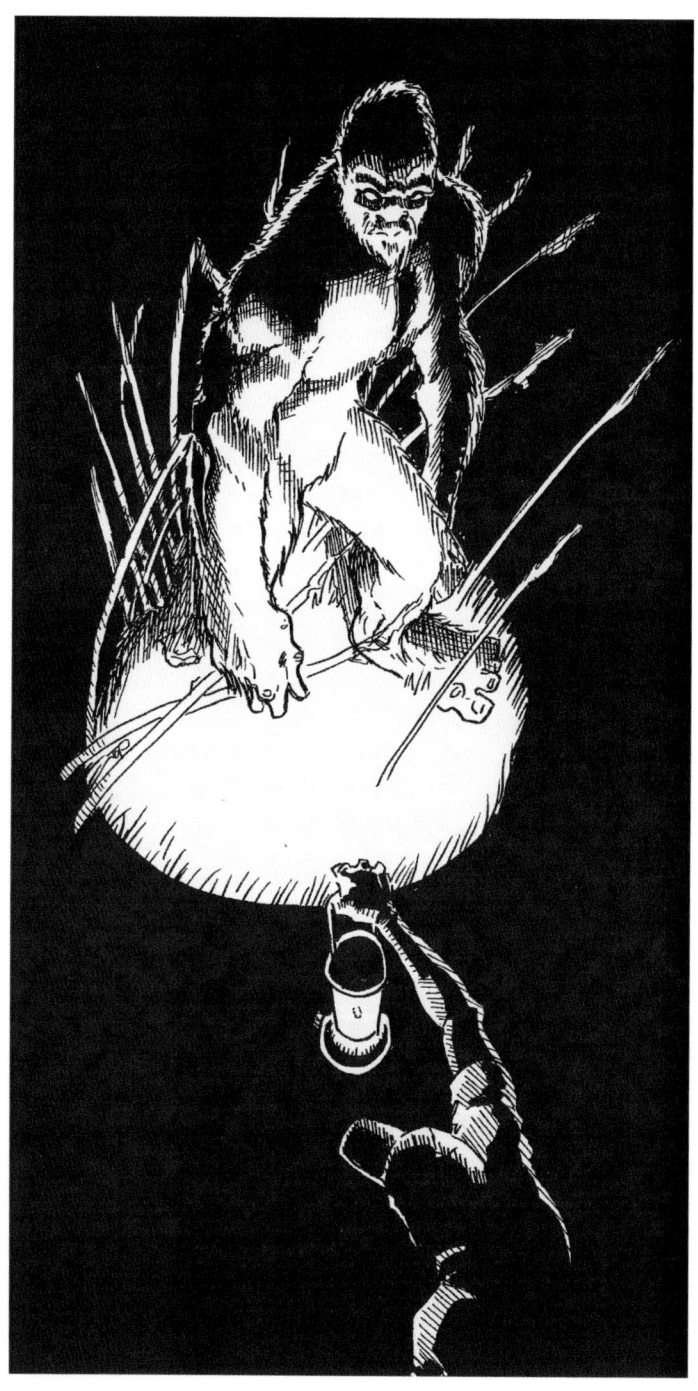
Re-creation of Bobby Grashel's encounter. *Illustration by the author.*

Amanda and Archie Halls were driving down Mobley Road near Beltline late one night when a creature ran in front of their truck. The couple described it as being an eight-foot-tall "very hairy man." They stopped so quickly that the television they were carrying in the bed of their truck was damaged—not something they were happy about, mind you. Their sighting occurred less than four miles from Bobby Grashel's and transpired at about the same time of night, just a few days later.

Though, clearly, the creature they all described was what we know as a Sasquatch today, instead of calling it a creature or monster, the firefighter used the name "goatman." He did this because his sighting occurred on the heels of the Lake Worth Monster event, so for Mr. Grashel, the Hallses and all of the inhabitants of the D/FW area, the furry figures that once bore so many names were all now goatman.

Greer Island's gruffy inhabitant and Jim Marrs didn't just give the local Sasquatch a new moniker—indeed that summer's antics had an immeasurable impact on the mythology of the Dallas/Fort Worth Metroplex. And a great example of this impact is found with one of D/FW's well-known devilish denizens, the goatman of Old Alton Bridge.

DENTON

The Goatman of Old Alton Bridge

William Smalling Peters negotiated a land contract with the Republic of Texas, and it was signed in 1841 by Peters's son-in-law Samuel Browning. The land grant created the Peters Colony, which (though the contract did need to be renegotiated, as there were mistakes made) would lay the groundwork for every town and county in North Texas. One of these initial settlements was known as Alton, and it started as the seat of Denton County. Though long-abandoned, there is one unique relic of Alton's heyday.

Between Teasley Lane and Copper Canyon Road in Argyle is a scenic greenspace that includes the Old Alton Bridge, which has been preserved and integrated into a popular hiking trail. The iron truss bridge was built by the King Iron Bridge Manufacturing Company in 1884 to connect the city of Copper Canyon with Denton. The bridge crosses Hickory Creek, which empties into Lake Lewisville, a man-made reservoir that was created by damming the Elm Fork of the Trinity River. Prior to the completion of

Old Alton Bridge, Argyle, Texas. *Courtesy of author.*

the Garza Dam in 1927, Hickory Creek was a tributary of the Trinity River and was used by those who founded the short-lived town of Alton to connect the community to the larger waterway.

On July 8, 1988, the bridge was added to the National Register of Historic Places, and it is frequented by tourists and hikers for its scenic beauty as well as its role in linking the Elm Fork–Pilot Knoll Hiking and Equestrian Trails. However, as you've no doubt guessed, Old Alton Bridge is not just known for its idyllic setting and beautiful photo opportunities. It has become a fairly popular paranormal attraction. Several decades of stories that the bridge itself is haunted by a hairy paranormal figure have made the retired bridge the subject of numerous articles and several television programs. It's difficult to pinpoint when the bridge fell into infamy, but for decades, people have told tales of rocks being thrown at them (in broad daylight no less) by towering furry figures of seven feet or greater that are hidden behind the tree line. Red glowing eyes on moonless nights and the stench of decaying flesh have also been reported, but cited far more often are accounts of spectral forms appearing on photographs or visitors being assaulted and scratched by an invisible phantom. What has really pushed Old Alton Bridge's goatman into the limelight are the stories told about his origins.

Drawing of the Old Alton Bridge Goatman. *Illustration by the author.*

The first tale is fairly straightforward: the bridge (notably beneath the structure) had served as a meeting point for witches and devil worshipers to practice their crafts. One fateful night, they sought to summon everyone's favorite dark lord, and he showed up. While perhaps not Beelzebub himself, this satyr-esque goatman was manifested on our mortal plane and now haunts the area to this very day. Interestingly, if the bridge wasn't used in the past to summon spirits and perform the dark arts, it is now. The legend of the goatman has inspired many to take their magical practices to the location; some have even taken to painting Ouija boards into the wooden planks that serve as the floor of the bridge.

The other stories are so similar that, from a folklore perspective, they should almost be considered the same story embellished by differing communities. The first is of a man who murdered his entire family and was hanged from the bridge for his heinous crimes. But this was no usual hanging. Due to his portly figure and a rope that was a bit too long, he was decapitated, and his head was lost in the stream. Legend has it that the ghostly body emerged from its grave in search of the misplaced cranium. On stumbling across a lost goat, the skull-less phantasm ripped the head clean off the unlucky beast and used it as a replacement. This spectral abomination continues to linger at the bridge, looking for its proper visage and wandering the land of the living for a prize it can never claim.

The alternative versions involve a Black goat herder named Oscar Washburn. Mr. Washburn moved to an area just north of the bridge and, over time, became beloved in the community and also fairly prosperous. He even eventually garnered the nickname Goatman. One day in 1938, he hung a sign from the bridge that read "This way to Goatman's." Local Ku Klux Klan members were enraged and jealous of his success. In one version of the story, the Klansmen kill the Washburn family and then frame him for

The Old Alton Bridge. *Courtesy of author.*

the crime. The local sheriff executes Mr. Washburn for the crimes he did not commit by hanging him from the Old Alton Bridge. The second version has the Washburn family being murdered and a farm burned to the ground by the KKK, after which poor Mr. Washburn is dragged by the Klansmen to the Old Alton Bridge, where he is viciously lynched. In both versions of the tale, the Klansmen looked over the edge of the bridge to find the noose empty and the body missing.

The third and final version of the story purportedly predates the bridge and tells of a runaway goat-herding slave by the name of Jack Kendall. As the tale goes, Mr. Kendall had escaped a particularly evil enslaver, only to be captured by a posse and then lynched from a tree that overlooked Hickory Creek.

It should be noted that all of the stories are variants on the theme of the hanging man family of urban legends, which are nearly universal in rural America. One of the most famous versions of this story comes from Meridian, Mississippi, and Stuckey's Bridge, which was originally constructed over the Chunky River in 1850 and rebuilt as an iron truss bridge (just like Old Alton Bridge) in 1901 by the Virginia Bridge and Iron Company. Stuckey's Bridge was said to be the spot where a former member of the infamous Dalton Gang, named Stuckey, was hanged for crimes committed after he left the Daltons. He had supposedly retired and opened an inn where he would kill and rob some of his visitors and then bury their bodies along the banks of the river. To this day, people claim that you can see his spectral form hanging from the bridge, hear the sound of his corpse hitting the water or see an old man with a light.

Like Old Alton Bridge's goatman, that Stuckey's Bridge story is by no means unique because people actually were executed by being hanged from bridges, particularly when mobs were involved. It should be noted that there was an out-of-work coal miner named Oscar Washburn who did live in Denton in the early 1900s. Unlike the story, however, he was a White man who died in June 1917, and there are no records of him being hanged for crimes (whether he committed them or not), nor that he ever tended flocks of goats. How Oscar became attached to the story is a matter of pure speculation and may ultimately be irrelevant because of what the story actually says about Denton County's evolving culture.

Folklore and urban legends are often societal tools designed with a moral or lesson to teach the young. Traveling at night was dangerous a century ago, particularly crossing an iron truss bridge over a river. Given that most children and teenagers often don't think of their own mortality when making decisions, sometimes a good ghost story of a killer's cursed and wandering spirit steps in to give them something to be afraid of. So, while the story of Old Alton Bridge's spirit was initially a useful story, as the era of the horse and buggy ended and the threat of careless children falling from the bridge was less of a problem, the story changed.

As the sixties came to a close and the name goatman was cemented in the D/FW cultural zeitgeist, Denton County's hanging man story evolved into the goatman. Gone was the psychopath righteously executed for his evil, and in his place was the troubled spirit of a good and kind Black man who was seeking justice for himself and his family. Even the story that claims to predate the bridge itself is about a runaway slave lynched for his attempt to gain the freedom denied him. No longer a simple ghost story, it has become an inescapable reminder of the horrors of the past. In many ways, Denton's goatman now stands as a testament to the crimes of the Ku Klux Klan and a reminder of the role racism has played in our society, serving as a touchstone for the county's growth from a collection of simple farming villages into a modern, integrated community.

Copy and Paste Monster

If the Old Alton goatman is simply a retelling of an older legend, then why do people claim to have seen or been assaulted by a creature, and what does the Greer Island goatman from 1969 have to do with it? Let's move aside the myth of the goatman's origins for a moment and look at what people have actually seen and then look again at what people say is seen or found at Old Alton Bridge.

This list was made by compiling all known written accounts and speaking with several other researchers who have made studies of the Old Alton Bridge.

ACTUALLY EXPERIENCED:
1. Photographs of ghosts or apparitions
2. Recordings that include EVP (electronic voice phenomena, where voices from unknown individuals who were not present appear on electronic recording devices)
3. Sensations of fear and being physically assaulted or scratched by unseen assailants

WHAT PEOPLE SAY:
1. Humanoid between seven and eight feet tall, covered in hair
2. Glowing red eyes
3. Encountered (often at night) in greenspaces near creeks or rivers
4. Throws rocks, tree branches, tires, trash, dead animals, et cetera at intrusive humans

Interestingly, the first set of phenomena (which is actually observed) is extremely common among haunted locations all around the world, but the second set (which are simply matters of lore and urban mythology) are not just common among Bigfoot encounters but are also identical to what was reported by Jim Marrs in his articles for the *Fort Worth Star Telegram* in 1969. The important clue to this is that it isn't just trash or rocks, but also tires that are thrown at people. What's happened is that the Greer Island goatman lore and mythology has merged with an older, preexisting ghost story and ultimately replaced the original primary figure of the older story.

Instead of being the Headless Man of Old Alton Bridge or the Hanging Man of Old Alton Bridge, the ghost is now the goatman of Old Alton Bridge, and that change allowed for a rewriting of his origin story. Now, it is important to state that there have been numerous Bigfoot sightings within just a few miles of the Old Alton Bridge, and the bridge is still along a creek largely protected by the green wall. It is entirely possible that, like in Cedar Hill, there were encounters with a Sasquatch shortly after 1969's Lake Worth event that initially inspired the locals to connect the two legends and ultimately led to the stories being merged.

We see a similar pattern of an older story being integrated with the Lake Worth event in another tragic goatman about as far south of Dallas as Denton is north of Dallas.

THE ITALY GOATMAN

Italy, Texas, was founded in 1879 toward the southern end of Ellis County, about fifteen miles south of Waxahachie. While cotton was the primary cash crop (and continues to be), Italy was also a huge producer of wheat and corn over the years, and its economy was initially bolstered by the railway that connected Dallas and Houston. The train brought not just a way for Italy residents to transport their crops to market but also an un-quieted spirit.

The old iron truss bridge that crosses Chamber's Creek in Italy, Texas. *Courtesy of author.*

Aside from the same Sasquatch-inspired lore, it is said that the sound of unseen goats can be heard along the train tracks while the spirit watches for those foolish enough to walk on the tracks. The reason given for this is that Italy's home-grown horned haunter is the spirit of a child who left his family's goat pen open, to tragic results.

The story goes that while the child tried to herd several goats off the tracks, he was tragically struck and killed by a train headed to Dallas. Sadly, there is ample reason to believe that the basic story of a child being struck on the train tracks was true, as numerous stories of this kind exist all over the United States from this time period. The reason for this is that following train tracks provided an easier (and safer) way of moving from one place to another if a road did not exist. But from time to time, younger children would not pay close enough attention and tragically lose their lives.

So, it is entirely likely that the original version of this story was inspired by an actual heartbreaking event in Italy's history. The real story starts off as a tale of caution but then becomes a ghost story to scare children from going on the tracks. Like the Old Alton Bridge stories though, the central figure of the myth is merged with the goatman lore due to potential Sasquatch contacts along Chambers Creek, and the story now includes the presence of lost goats to not only explain why this "ghost" is now a goatman but also to serve as a reminder to the rural children of the area to take care in performing their chores.

Note: Navarro County's Richland-Chambers Reservoir, located around twenty-one miles south of Ennis and thirty-two miles east of Italy, was created by impounding water from Chambers Creek (along which Italy was established) and Richland Creek. Richland-Chambers Reservoir is the third largest reservoir in Texas by surface area and is the center for a number of Bigfoot sightings due to its vast greenspaces and low human population.

Old Foamy

Cleburne, Johnson County

If you find yourself driving through Cleburne (on the southern fringe of the metroplex) late at night, you might want to visit Old Foamy Road and the small low-water bridge you'll find there. According to Richard Dickerson, archivist for the Johnson County Historical Commission Museum, as the waters of Buffalo Creek would pass under the (original) bridge, the waters would foam due to the soaps or other contaminates that used to be found in the water, hence the name of the road. But the bridge's former reaction to detergent isn't the reason for the visit. Local legend tells of a goatman that is summoned by honking the horn of your car three times at midnight. Once bidden, the mysterious creature is alleged to assault the vehicle by throwing dead carcasses of pets and wild animals or even attacking the car itself by leaping on the hood of the automobile. Described as a seven-foot-tall hairy humanoid with goat's horns and cloven feet, the goatman known as Old Foamy has been a staple of Johnson County's lore since the late sixties, and this ritual is an important coming of age prank for the younger citizens of the area.

Now, why teens find the idea of summoning a trash-tossing monster to scratch and dent their car appealing is a mystery to me, but it is a mystery that surrounds all of the hooved horrors haunting the bridges and cemeteries of North Texas. Interestingly, in many ways, Cleburne's resident cloven recluse is a carbon copy of Denton's, which means one

Old Foamy Bridge. "Old Foamy" is just the worst name for such a menacing mythological creature. He should look into suing someone. *Courtesy of author.*

either was inspired by the other or they are inspired by the same earlier mythology (perhaps even a bit of both). The theme of summoning a ghost (like the Old Alton Bridge goatman) or a potential devil (also like the Old Alton Bridge goatman) by knocking on a bridge or honking a car horn thrice is fairly common in modern mythology.

After all, how do you summon the ghost of Bloody Mary? You say her name three times in a mirror. The ghost of little Edna Collins is conjured by driving to Edna Collins Bridge in Indiana, turning off your car and then honking or flashing your lights three times. That certainly sounds familiar. All of these nearly universal urban traditions might be born of real occult practices going back to the ancient Greek veneration of Hecate, the "three-fold" goddess.

Given this connection to the occult, it does need to be noted that there is a story that has been circulated among the residents of Cleburne that involves a car full of bored teenagers who decided to test the Old Foamy ritual one Saturday night. The story goes that the kids pulled up to the bridge, rolled down their windows, cut off the engine (just as they had been instructed) and made the requisite three honks. Nothing happened. The group began to laugh and tease one another as a mysterious figure emerged from the dark in the rear window. The friends turned in terror to see a black-cloaked figure wearing a cow skull as a mask approaching the car. The driver was able to restart his car just in time for the kids to escape the situation, but as the driver was focused on keeping the car from going into a ditch while speeding down the small farm road, his friends noticed numerous Satanists decked out in similar apparel on either side of the road as they sped away. Obviously, the kids made it out to tell the tale.

As frightening and universal as this tale is, Cleburne resident Michael Turner (who I interviewed while he was buying a pack of cigarettes from a gas station/bait store just a few miles from the infamous bridge) had the following to say: "I've lived about a mile from Old Foamy for years, and I've done the honking thing to scare a couple of girlfriends.…The only goatmen I've ever seen are other locals who need to quit drinking."

A note about the history of this quiet and unassuming city: Incorporated in 1871, Cleburne was the site of the drafting of the Cleburne Demands in 1886 by the Texas Farmers' Alliance. The Cleburne Demands were the first official salvo in the agrarian revolts of the late nineteenth century. The alliance would eventually help create the People's Party, from which modern American populism was born. The ambiguous policies of American populism can easily be traced to the alliance's notoriously vague goals:

> *No man…can give a perfect definition of the purposes of the Farmers' Alliance; and he who attempts a definition simply gives his own personal conception of the subject, which may be more or less valuable, according to whether his field of observation and his accuracy of judgment are good or otherwise. In a broad sense, the purposes of the Farmers' Alliance… cover today a remedy for every evil known to exist and afflict farmers and other producers, and in the future should cover every contingency that may arise, presenting evil to be combatted by means of organization; they are accumulative and ever changing, as the enemy assumes a new guise.*
>
> *C.W. Macune, Southern Alliance leader, 1891*

Cleburne was also the birthplace of the alliance's replacement, the Texas State Federation of Labor, which was created in 1900.

Creature of Copper Canyon

On the evening of January 21, 2008, researcher Lance Oliver and his wife, Mary, witnessed the amber glow of a chevron-shaped UFO dancing across

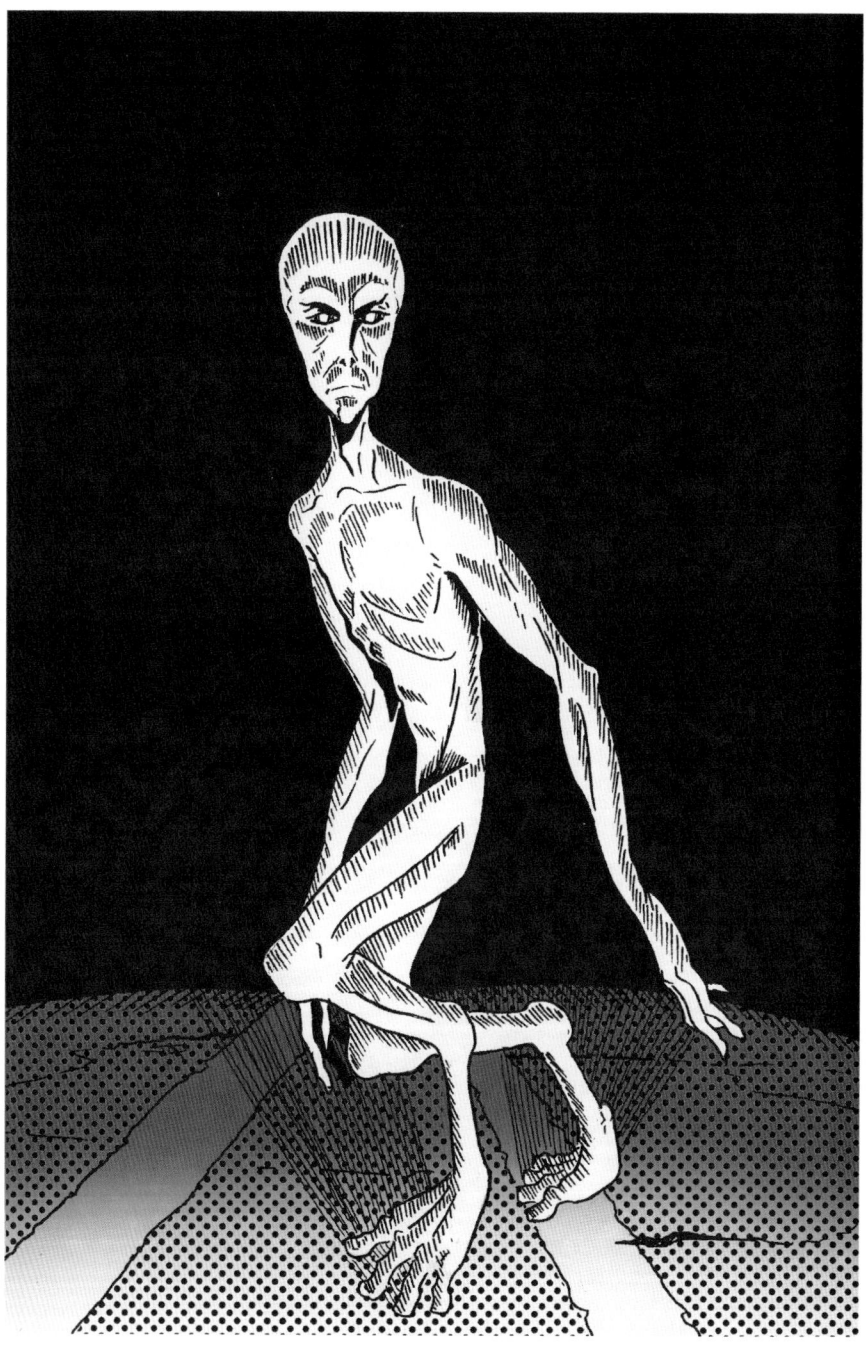

Rendering of the Copper Canyon Creature based on drawings made by Todd of Bob's description. *Courtesy of author.*

the Denton sky "like a stone skipping across the surface of the water," as Mr. Oliver described it. This evening took an even stranger turn for an individual Lance calls "Bob" in order to protect his identity.

Bob was dropping off a friend of his named "Todd" after watching a late-night film and decided to take Copper Canyon Road to save on gas because he was driving a large truck, and unleaded gasoline was nearly three dollars a gallon at the time. It was around 2:00 a.m. when Bob made the sharp turn east to cross over the train tracks. He continued down Copper Canyon Road and slammed on the brakes harder than he ever had before. Less than twenty feet in front of him, standing perfectly still in the light of his truck's high beams, was a five-foot-tall hairless creature. The strange oblong head, long spindly arms and dog-like legs astonished Bob, who sat there stunned until the creature effortlessly bounded across the street and turned back to look at Bob from the tree line before disappearing into the woods. Bob could tell that the creature turned to look at him because his eyes had a cat-like yellow reflective glow. As soon as the creature was gone, Bob floored it home and locked every door he had.

Several days after the event, Bob related the encounter to Todd, who, as he was an artist, drew the entity his friend had seen. Both the story and image were reported to Mr. Oliver, who verified the date using Bob's movie ticket stub, which he still had. Bob has never seen the creature again, nor is there anything directly connecting this elongated thing to the UFO seen just a few hours earlier. To make matters more complicated, the area where Bob saw this creature was less than five thousand feet from Old Alton Bridge. Copper Canyon Road is where the bridge was before its retirement. Was this an alien visitor, the actual entity on which the goatman of Old Alton Bridge is based or a juvenile Bigfoot sick with mange? I'll leave that to you.

Dallas Demons

As a native Dallasite, I can confirm that perhaps the funniest thing about the city of Dallas is the argument over the origins of its name. Everyone seems to agree that the Spanish claimed the area from the Caddo tribes that had set up satellite villages along the Trinity River and its tributaries. (The Caddo nation—the westernmost arm of the Mississippian Empire—was centered in deep East Texas and Louisiana and had satellite villages strewn across the waterways of Texas to facilitate trade.) Then the French took it from them and on and on it went until 1836 and the creation of the Republic of Texas. With the sovereign state encouraging expansion, John Neely Bryan, guided by a Cherokee named Ned, claimed his stake in 1839 and established, in 1841, a permanent settlement named Dallas. No one argues any of these events, but they do argue how Dallas became the name. You'd think he would have named it after himself, but instead, Mr. Bryan either named it after a small Scottish village from which his family originated or after the United States' eleventh vice president, George Mifflin Dallas, as an attempt to curry some favor with the American government. There is also the theory that the settlement was named after Vice President Dallas's brother, Commodore Alexander James Dallas, who died in 1844, also designed to win brownie points from the United States.

While the real origin of the city's name may never be known, what is indisputable is that Dallas County was incorporated in 1846 (a year after the United States annexed Texas) and quickly became an important economic center due to its location along the Trinity River. The village of Dallas would become so important that a decade later (February 2, 1856, to be precise), it was incorporated as the city of Dallas, Texas. Though the Dallas area would experience a boom after the Civil War, during the Great Westward Migration, it was the arrival of the Houston & Texas Central Railroad (H&TC) in 1872 (the same train that ran through Italy) that really kicked off the city's economic dominance. Now the cotton and pecans from the surrounding areas had, for the first time, rapid and reliable transportation to markets in Houston for transport to the textile mills in the North or even international markets.

This post–Civil War economic and population expansion brought many important individuals and families to the area, including a dentist, gambler and gunslinger named John Henry "Doc" Holliday. Holliday, seeking drier climates to ease the symptoms of his tuberculosis, set up shop in September 1873 at 56 Elm Street but left in 1875 after a shootout with a bartender. He would eventually find himself in the Bee Hive Saloon at Fort Griffin (near current-day Albany, Texas, about 160 miles west of Dallas) around October 1877. This is where he would encounter deputy U.S. marshal Wyatt Earp.

Dallas continued to grow in wealth, due in no small part to the enormous expansion of cotton production in the surrounding areas, and in geographic size by annexing the surrounding towns like Oak Cliff (in 1901). In fact, the fifteen-story Praetorian Building, constructed in 1909, was the first skyscraper west of the Mississippi. By 1914, Dallas was the seat of the Eleventh Federal Reserve District, and by the mid-1930s, it became the central distribution hub for the oil discovered in Kilgore (about 120 miles east), Oklahoma, the Texas panhandle and the Permian basin in West Texas and Southeast New Mexico. While the surrounding agricultural and oil and coal production drove Dallas's prosperity, it was World War II that really pushed Dallas (and the entire metroplex) to the forefront industrially and set the stage for Dallas to become the heart of the "Silicon Prairie."

Note: By 1925, Texas accounted for one-third of the nation's cotton production, and the area served by Dallas's railways (about a one hundred–mile radius) was responsible for 31 percent of Texas's cotton harvest. Ellis County (the county immediately south of Dallas) was the top cotton-producing county in the world during this time, with much of this cotton coming from the small town of Avalon, Texas, which is located just east of Italy between Chambers Creek and Big Onion Creek.

During World War II, Texas became strategically important due to its central location in the country and abundance of natural resources and agricultural produce. With over 750,000 Texans serving in uniform, and many sent overseas, nearly 1.5 million people descended on the state for military training or construction of military vehicles and weaponry—or just to help keep the state's farms, wells and mines running. Aside from the military manufacturing facilities that continued to turn out equipment for the Cold War, the Korean War and other military engagements, one of the big reasons Dallas became a leader in the digital and communications revolutions was a small company named Geophysical Service Incorporated (GSI).

GSI was founded in the 1930s and built seismic equipment used in finding and developing oil wells to serve the needs of the growing petroleum market. Given the similarity between seismic geological equipment and the technology needed for submarine detection, GSI was tapped to produce electronics used by the U.S. Signal Corps and the U.S. Army and Navy. By 1951, GSI became Texas Instruments (TI for locals) and went on to invent the integrated circuit (the microchip) by 1958. And yes, it invented and continues to build those giant calculators with all the weird symbols that you had to use in high school.

Yet for all of Dallas's prosperity—the manufacturing plants, railways, highways and omnipresent concrete sprawl—it is a city with a number of ghosts—well, perhaps the word "demons" is more accurate.

The Lady of White Rock Lake and Her Pet Goatman

Located just five miles from the center of Downtown Dallas is White Rock Lake—a reservoir created in 1911 with the completion of the White Rock Dam. As you may have already surmised, the White Rock Creek, a tributary of the Trinity River, was named for the white limestone into which the creek had cut deeply. While the reservoir is no longer used as a source of drinking water for the city of Dallas, it remains a popular park for jogging, picnicking and even sailing, which would have seemed quite odd to the original inhabitants. The area was originally a collection of farms owned by the Daniel family as early as the 1830s. After the Civil War, Thomas Walker Daniel invited his friend by the name of Cox to migrate to the area to farm the vast, and largely empty, land surrounding a small town called Dallas. Over the years, a few more pioneer families came to the area, including the McCommases, whose name is common around east Dallas streets and locations (most notably McCommas Bluff). The Daniels, Coxes and other

White Rock Lake, Dallas. *Courtesy of author.*

early White Rock Creek settlers were laid to rest at Cox Cemetery, which still exists to this day.

Like most lakes, sadly, White Rock Lake has known many suicides and tragic boating accidents, which has led to many tales of ghosts and apparitions appearing and then vanishing just as quickly. The most famous of these tales is the Lady of White Rock Lake. The story first hit circulation in 1943 with Anne Clark's "The Ghost of White Rock," which was published in *Backwoods to Border*, a publication of the Texas Folklore Society. The story is as familiar of a ghost story as they come: a young couple got into their car after a day of fun at White Rock Lake and turned on the headlights. The couple was startled by a woman standing in front of the car wearing a white dress that was dripping wet from being submerged in the lake. She told the couple that she was in a boating accident and that though the others who were with her were fine, she needed a ride to her house in Oak Cliff. She gave them the address and then climbed in, only to disappear, leaving a small puddle of water. Confused, the lovers drove to the address the mysterious maiden had given and found an older man who told them that they were the third couple in three weeks to have that same account. He then informed them that his daughter had drowned at White Rock Lake while boating the month before.

Later, in 1953, the story was repeated and embellished in Frank X. Tolbert's *Neiman-Marcus, Texas: The Story of the Proud Dallas Store*. In his account, the story remains the same, except the girl never explains how she came to be there or why her dress is drenched. Additionally, the couple that finds the wayward spirit notes that her dress *must* be from Neiman-Marcus because of how nice it was prior to her disappearing. The home they travel to is much closer, in the Lakewood neighborhood off of Gaston Avenue, and instead of a boating accident the previous month, the girl had died tragically three years earlier when she fell from a pier at White Rock Lake.

The punchline of Tolbert's version of the story, of course, was how the drowned young girl only wore dresses from Neiman-Marcus. The inclusion of this is element was a clear attempt to usurp the urban legend and transform it into a marketing ploy, although I don't know why Mr. Tolbert (or Neiman-Marcus for that matter) would assume that a ghost wearing dresses from a particular store would make someone *want* to buy clothes from said store, but there you have it.

While you could forgive people who write off any ghost stories about the area as nonsense, every Dallas native knows and recognizes that White Rock Lake is a beautiful and haunted place. This sentiment was shared by noted researcher Nick Redfern after he lived in the area for several years. In an article, he wrote that White Rock Lake was "without a doubt the strangest place I have ever lived." Intertwined with these tales of phantom women, although seemingly unrelated, are accounts of a satyr-like creature known as the goatman. Though less well known than his Denton counterpart, the goatman of White Rock Lake does have something the Old Alton Bridge version does not: eyewitnesses.

Unlike the other goatmen, who are urban legends born of a merging of the reports from the Lake Worth event and an older ghost mythology, Dallas's devilish denizen is a bit more of an exhibitionist than the other specters. Those who have seen him describe the creature as a seven-foot-tall man with either a greenish pallor or yellow, jaundiced skin. His body is covered in coarse goat-like fur and possesses both goat horns and hooves, just like a satyr from Greek mythology. There are claims that people see red glowing eyes from behind the tree line and that he throws tires and trash at people. Some have even heard the sounds of goats when none are present. Obviously, these are aspects of the surrounding goatmen lore that have been placed on this all-too-observable figure.

Our first account occurred after midnight in the fall of 1989. Matthew Colvard and a small group of friends decided to walk off the night's festivities by exploring the White Rock Lake jogging path and looking for the aforementioned phantom female who haunts the waters of the reservoir. They were walking around the northern end of the lake, not too far from the Cox Cemetery, when Matthew Colvard's date ran ahead. She turned around and began giving the group a hard time for being slow, but before

Dallas Demons, Fort Worth Goatmen & Other Terrors of the Trinity River

The goatman, as seen by Matthew Colvard and his group from 1989. *Illustration by the author.*

she could complete her playful jab, she screamed in terror. Taken aback at first, Matthew and the rest of the group realized that their companion was reacting to something behind them, so they turned around.

As it was backlit from the streetlamp, Mr. Colvard couldn't see any fine details, but at the edge of the tree line, less than thirty feet from them, stood the infamous goatman.

"He was around seven, maybe eight foot tall." Matthew noted, "The light was behind him, so he was basically just a dark silhouette with red glowing eyes, but I could clearly see his horns on the top of his head and the goat legs he had. He just stood there looking at us, but we were freaking out. Next thing I know, we're all running back to the car and got out of there as fast as we could."

Aside from unexpected cardio (and an aversion to being at White Rock Lake after dark), the group escaped unscathed and with an interesting anecdote. While it could be argued that Matthew and his group were simply the victims of an elaborate hoax, it should be pointed out that pulling a prank like this, particularly in Dallas, Texas, is a good way to get yourself hurt. Even though carrying a concealed weapon was not legal in Texas until 1995, it was not uncommon (particularly after dark), and anyone who knew enough about Dallas to pull a prank like this would also be aware of this fact. That being said, it certainly isn't impossible to imagine some high school or college kids ignoring this and putting a great deal of effort into creating a costume that could fool people at night. This is why we should discuss Sandy Grace's encounter with the beast.

The story of Ms. Grace was recorded by researcher Nick Redfern and recounted in his work *Memoirs of a Monster Hunter*. Sandy was using the popular jogging path that surrounds White Rock Lake—something she did often. It was around 2:00 p.m. in August 2001, when Ms. Grace felt overwhelmed with an unprovoked sense of fear. Not prone to panic attacks, Ms. Grace was confused by her sudden onset of anxiety, as there was nothing that she could see that would cause this reaction, until out from behind the tree line stepped the goatman.

Stopping in her tracks at seeing this monstrous figure, Ms. Grace's unnatural panic turned into completely justified terror when the cloven creature deliberately approached her. It walked slowly toward her, bearing what Mr. Redfern described as "a malevolent, sneering grin on its face." Just as the seven-foot-tall satyr got within fifteen feet of the frightened jogger, it kneeled down and disappeared in a blinding flash of light. Mr. Redfern recorded that the witness was certain that she had not hallucinated the event

The goatman, as seen by Sandy Grace. *Illustration by the author.*

and that it was as real as anything that she had ever run into; however, she was also certain that the creature she saw could not be native to White Rock Lake or even this plane of existence.

Coming face-to-face with what appears to be the same creature that stalked Mr. Colvard's group a dozen years earlier, Sandy described the creature in much the same way as Matthew: unusually tall, possessing two horns on his head and having goat-like legs.

Clearly, these two eyewitnesses were both describing a creature that is not a Bigfoot and seemingly comes straight out of a fantasy film—or Greek mythology. It is here that Nick Redfern keenly pointed out that the word "panic" is derived from the name of the Greek god Pan. It was believed that if disturbed from his midday nap, Pan would let out a cry that would cause the surrounding herds of livestock to stampede out of fear. This sense of sudden and total fear was called *panikos* in Greek and became "panic" in English. Mr. Redfern did ask Ms. Grace how often she'd had a sudden panic attack in her life, and she confirmed that this was both the first and last panic attack she'd ever had.

Just a quick note that seemed out of place in the story but is a fun bit of trivia you can use to impress people at parties: The Lady of White Rock Lake was the inspiration for the Country Gentlemen's "Bringing Mary Home," a song written by the group's mandolin player, John Duffey. The song made the Billboard Country Chart in 1965 and has become a bluegrass staple covered by many musicians, including Ricky Skaggs and Mac Wiseman. Duffey and the rest of the Country Gentlemen were inducted into the International Bluegrass Music Hall of Honor in 1996.

The Goatman Goes Traveling

The Pleasant Grove Phantom

Claudia Marines was four years old when her mother, Delores, became very sick, and Claudia became her full-time caregiver. While her father was working or taking care of the house, Claudia would help her mother use the restroom, take her diabetes medication and massage her legs. Given their young age and Claudia's role as her mother's primary caregiver, she shared her room with her brother and mother while her father slept on the couch. Every night, the trio would tune their handheld radio to an AM station that broadcasted old radio plays and crack the room's lone window open a little bit to allow for a slight breeze.

It was a cool spring night in 1989 when the trio woke to the sound of a woman at their window screaming to be let in: "He's after me! Let me in!" Though the woman implored Claudia and her mother to open the window, given the dangerous nature of the neighborhood, it had been designed to only open a few inches.

Claudia yelled, "Come around the front because we can't let you in through the window!" She and her brother woke up their father, who found no one at the front door. Fearing for the woman's safety, he checked around the house and found no sign of the woman who had woken his family.

After locking up the house, he found Delores in the farthest corner of her room from the window, holding the children and frantically praying

The goatman, as seen by Claudia Marines. *Illustration by the author.*

the rosary while staring out the window. Before he could fully ask her what she was looking at, he saw the glowing red eyes of a creature standing a mere thirty feet away. At the end of their backyard was Pleasant Branch Creek, a concrete drainage ditch that carries runoff water to Prairie Creek (a tributary of the Trinity River, just like White Rock Creek). This concrete ditch is around six feet deep, and the creature stood a full head and shoulders out of it. Terrified by the creature's size, oblong head and massive build, Claudia's father pulled his family into the main living room to sleep that night.

The Dallas Demon

It was 3:00 a.m. in the summer of 2018 when, returning from grocery shopping at their local twenty-four-hour Walmart, the Orozcos, Sara and Edgar, had the first of several encounters with the goatman. With their son asleep in the back of their car, the Orozcos turned into the alley behind their house and pulled

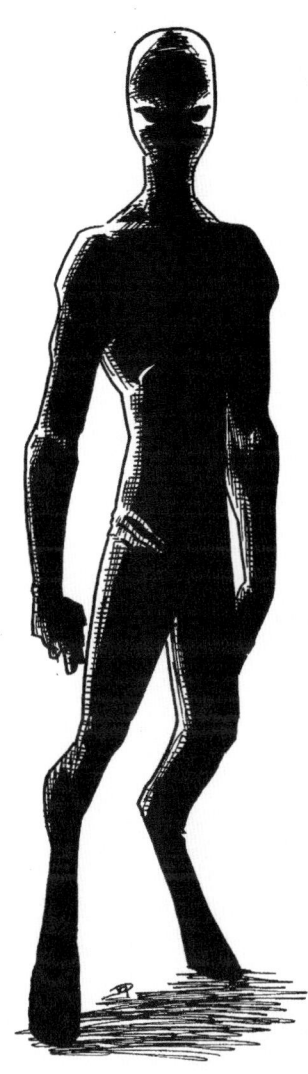

The goatman, as seen by Sara and Edgar's son. *Illustration by the author.*

into their driveway. Strangely, the garage door didn't respond to the remote. While Edgar was trying to get the garage door opened, Sara looked down the alley and noticed that the streetlamp at the end of the alley, where the creek runs through the neighborhood, also wasn't working. On closer inspection, she realized that the lamp was actually working, but there was an extremely tall and dark creature blocking the light. She described it as slender with an elongated head, long arms and very long fingers. Edgar didn't see the creature but did note that he couldn't see the lamppost, which was strange because even if the lamp was off, the ambient light from the neighbors' lights should have at least allowed him to see the post.

After they manually opened the garage, Sara rushed the trio into the house. She described what she saw to her husband, who initially ignored the observation, suggesting that perhaps she had briefly fallen asleep and dreamed the encounter. The next morning, as they were driving to church, they headed down the same alley. As they drove past the lamppost, they both noticed a burned area on it and on the ground where Sara had seen the creature. As they continued down the alley, the car was hit by a large, unseen force, causing it to shake and tip.

This startled Edgar, who exclaimed, "What the heck did we hit?" He quickly got out of the car, fearing he had hit a large dog or even a child that he hadn't seen. Frantically searching under and behind his car, Edgar found no injured animal, child or large pothole. There was also no damage to his car. There was nothing. This "nothing" that Edgar hit would come back to frighten him when, over the next several nights, their son came into Sara and Edgar's bedroom saying that the "Black Man" was staring into his bedroom.

At first, Edgar thought his son meant one of the neighbors had gotten into their backyard, so he began checking their video surveillance but found no one on camera. Sara asked their son to draw the figure he saw while Edgar was checking the system. The child drew the same dark creature Sara had seen. Both parents were confused by their son's drawing since he had been asleep at the time of the initial encounter, and both had agreed to not discuss it with their son so that they didn't disturb him. For several nights, the creature appeared and stood in front of the window, staring at the child. Even with the thick curtains drawn, he could sense the creature returning night after night until it ended with no more reason than when it began.

The Goatmen throughout History

The creatures seen by Claudia and Sara may not seem connected to the hybridized satyr seen by Sandy and Matthew; however, not only did all of these observations occur within easy walking distance of White Rock Lake, but they also involved waterways that connect to White Rock Creek. While the idea of a seemingly impossible creature roaming around Dallas sounds like something out of a bad horror movie, I should point out that similar creatures have been described all throughout human history, appearing in many different cultures across eons. While we see depictions of spirits and gods as horned or antlered humanoid figures in cave art and carvings in Europe and North America, the best place to start our journey is Mesopotamia. The sands of western Asia may seem a strange place to begin, but the first goatman recorded in human history comes from the ancient *Epic of Gilgamesh*.

Aside from D/FW and Mesopotamia both encompassing the thirty-second parallel north, Mesopotamia also shared the metroplex's dependency on two major rivers for survival. In many ways, the Fertile Crescent created by the Tigris and the Euphrates is similar to the watersheds of the Trinity and Brazos that make agriculture possible for North Texas. It was along the banks of the rivers in the Fertile Crescent that the Sumerian, Akkadian and Babylonian empires emerged. Given that the Sumerians were the first to develop writing (or so most scholars currently believe), it should come as no surprise that the earliest epic poem was found buried in the sands of what is now Iraq. The *Epic of Gilgamesh*, thought to have been written around 1800

BC and believed to be mankind's earliest extant written work, tells the story of the selfish and arrogant king Gilgamesh.

To correct Gilgamesh's arrogance and make him a better king, the gods shape the wild man Enkidu from clay. He is raised by animals and removed from human civilization. He is seen as an embodiment of nature that first opposed Gilgamesh and is then civilized by the king and becomes his servant and friend. After Enkidu's death, the result of injuries he received during a battle with the monster Humbaba, Gilgamesh sets off to learn the secret of immortality. Though the king does manage to obtain this secret, it is ultimately stolen by a snake, prompting Gilgamesh to return to Uruk as a changed and benevolent ruler. In the final tablet of Gilgamesh's story, Enkidu is allowed to leave the underworld and emerges from a crack in the earth as a ghost that converses with Gilgamesh.

Gawain MacGregor, self-described shaman mentioned earlier in the chapter titled "What Is Texas Bigfoot?," calls his religious belief "Enkiduism" after the mythological figure from the *Epic of Gilgamesh*. Mr. MacGregor considers Enikdu to be connected to the Sasquatch phenomenon, due to an encounter with what he believes to be a Bigfoot that he claims to have had after a vision quest.

While the epic is a fictional story, depictions of the wild man Enkidu from a period that predates the written story render him as a human with the horns and legs of a bull. This strange human combined with cattle theme is repeated with the satyrs and fauns of Greek and Roman mythology, which, though originally depicted as humans with the ears and tail of a donkey, evolved over time to include donkey or goat legs. Perhaps the most famous satyr imagery is the aforementioned god Pan. Deity of the wild and shepherds, Pan was often rendered as a human with goat legs and horns. Several of the most famous statues of Pan were uncovered in Pompeii and give the deity a human face that is seemingly in transition to that of a goat, pushing the idea that this pagan god is more animal than human.

As a god of nature, he was worshipped in natural grottoes, which are caves near bodies of water. These grottoes are prone to flooding and are often formed in limestone (remember that Dallas sits on a solid bed of limestone) when the water dissolves the carbonate in the rock matrix and creates a cave. It was believed that Pan danced in the woods to music he played on pan pipes, which are named for him and you may recognize as the multi-stemmed flute played by the beloved fictional character Peter Pan. These joyous romps are derived from an earlier and more sinister origin, though, because while Pan was revered as a god and Roman, fauns were considered symbols of fertility, and satyrs were feared by travelers who had to traverse empty and uncivilized places.

British classical scholar Martin Litchfield West connects the satyr to Proto-Indo-European mythology, in which human/animal hybrids were seen as mischievous supernatural figures that haunt wild places (often seen dancing) and trick travelers into losing their way. In Professor West's opinion, both traditions seem to emerge from the same older traditions, and he notes that satyrs are similar in appearance to the Indo-European *lešiy* ("leshy" in English) of Slavic mythology. This spirit was a temperamental fairy to some and was seen by others as evil because he would cause sojourners to get lost in the woods. While causing someone to lose their way seems innocent enough in the modern day, it could easily lead to death by starvation or attack by wild animal several thousand years ago.

The idea of supernatural goatmen haunting wild and untamed places wasn't limited to the Greeks or other Indo-European cultures. They can be found in the Hebrew Bible as well. Though evidence of this is not as abundant as that of the satyr or Enkidu, many scholars believe that the Hebrew śěʾîrîm (we transliterate that as "sheydim") were goat-like demons worshipped by heretical Israelites and are mentioned in Leviticus 17:7, 2 Chronicles 11:15 and Isaiah 13:21. Isaiah's account even discusses these goat demons dancing in empty places.

So, for the ancient traveler, a satyr was a supernatural threat to be avoided and feared, and their Indo-European origins seem to make them similar to wisps or fairies. A modern understanding of this concept would be an evil spirit, demon or even vengeful ghost. In one way or another, people have feared and worshipped these peculiar paranormal caprinae since the beginning of time, and the themes echo throughout centuries in the mythology of ancient cultures, fairy tales told by our forefathers and urban legends of the D/FW Metroplex.

La Mujer Lechuza, Also Known as the Lechuza of Oak Cliff

When discussing the things that go bump in the night, particularly in Texas, one must inevitably address the Lechuza. For those unfamiliar with Spanish, the word *lechuza* does mean "owl" (a barn or screech owl usually), but it is also the colloquial name for a feared magical being. According to the story La Mujer Lechuza, there was a witch who transformed into a giant owl at night to seek her victims, usually children. There are regional variations to the tale, obviously, and it shares many similarities with another Latin American vampiric female known as La Chorca. While often presented as an urban legend native to the Rio Grande Valley and northern Mexican territories, in truth, the Lechuza goes as far back as Homer's *Iliad*—if not further. To understand the connection, though, we need to turn to Angelica Lopez and her encounter with the fearsome monstrosity.

While a Christian and avid churchgoer now, Angelica's life did not start that way. Ms. Lopez was born into a long line of *curandera*, female shamans who use naturopathy and witchcraft to heal and treat sicknesses or curse those who have wronged them. Angelica's family practiced (some still do) a synchronistic and polytheistic mysticism similar to Santeria, and after her parents died, she went to live with her aunt, who served as a curandera for the Oak Cliff area of South Dallas.

"She was decked out in this apron that was covered in pockets," Ms. Lopez recalled of her aunt. "They were full of little bottles of holy water and herbs and charms; anything she used on a regular basis to cast spells or break curses." Constantly picked on for being a witch—despite her avoidance of

Dallas Demons, Fort Worth Goatmen & Other Terrors of the Trinity River

The Lechuza, as described by Angelica. *Illustration by the author.*

the craft—Angelica would often awaken to dead chickens in the front yard or rows of holy water, black salt or redbrick dust. It is sufficient to say that she grew up familiar with the occult, but what happened to her in 1997 would change her life forever.

As a teenager, Ms. Lopez would sneak out at night and hang out with her friends at the nearby McDonald's, which kept its dining room open until midnight. Since many of the employees were her friends, their little group could stay in the safety of the building while they cleaned and locked up for the evening, but this also meant that she and her best friend would walk home around at one o'clock in the morning—after most of the lights from local businesses were shut off. This was only made worse when she crossed Twelfth Street because it was here that the pair entered a residential area full of trees, and given the hour, most porch lights were off for the night.

"It got even spookier," Angelica noted, "after this building on the street we took got converted to Section 8 housing. You never knew if you were going to run into some dude that was high or drunk; which, looking back on it, was a really stupid thing to be doing at our age." But on the evening in question, she and her friend noticed that the Oak Cliff evening was much darker and quieter than usual, "like someone had turned off everything. It was weirdly quiet." At least it was quiet until they heard the crash of some large and unseen creature in a nearby tree.

"It was like a bird the size of a horse landed in the tree next to us," Angelica recalled. "The whole tree shook violently, and branches were breaking, which we thought was weird but figured it was safer for us just to head home instead of figuring out what did it." As the pair hurried home, the unknown creature leapt from one tree to the next, crashing on each one like a sledgehammer but always staying behind them. After the fifth tree, Angelica's friend ran off, saying that the monster must be after her since her family was full of witches.

"I better not be dead in the morning, you punk---!" she yelled. Angelica turned to face her unknown stalker and pulled out the pocketknife she carried while traversing Oak Cliff's less friendly streets. It is important to note that at this time Ms. Lopez wasn't certain what she was facing. She could tell that this wasn't a squirrel or cat but didn't believe it to be anything more than some drug addict following two girls home. After it became clear that whatever was following her was not interested in face-to-face conflict, she turned and kept walking toward her house. When she was only a few houses away, and the trees were too few or small to hold the creature's weight, it flew over her to land in the oak tree in front of her.

"I couldn't see it yet, and I couldn't tell how big it was, but the wings clearly went from one side of the street to the other. I didn't really see a form either, just black darkness against the night sky." It is important to note that even though this was a dark residential area, it was not far from numerous light sources, so young Ms. Lopez's night sky was more like a dark purple than the black starlight one finds farther away from downtown Dallas. "It was at that moment that I realized that there was no sound, like at all. No thumping from the music from the gang hang out a block over, no dogs, not even the sound of the cars—nothing. I was only seven houses from home, and I could feel this thing watching me, so my fight-or-flight kicked in, and it said run!

"I don't know if it stayed in that tree or if it started moving on the houses because all I could focus on was getting in my aunt's house as fast as I could. There was a window with some milk crates that I used to sneak in and out, but that plan was no longer an option." Angelica used her knife to bang on the windows to wake up someone in the house to let her in the front door.

At this point, the thing landed in the old oak tree in her aunt's yard. She could hear the limbs creaking and bending above her as her aunt opened the door and looked to the tree immediately. "She started throwing holy water and charms at the thing in the tree and told me not to look…but my dumb--- turned and looked. What I saw was what looked like a giant owl—much, much larger than any owl should be, like bigger than a person. It was black and brown with white on the tips of the wings, but it had a woman's face. Everything about this creature was bird—an unimaginably large and heavy bird—except for the face. The eyes had an orange eye shine, but it had a woman's mouth and nose."

Her aunt was cussing at the creature and praying to get rid of it while Angelica quickly crawled in the house. She was ordered to take off her clothes and take a shower so that her aunt could perform cleansing spells. While washing off the egg yolk and other occult material, Angelica's aunt took her clothes and favorite Doc Martins to be burned to remove whatever attracted the Lechuza in the first place.

It was in this silence, while she was alone, that she could hear the tapping of the Lechuza's talons on the glass. The creature tapped on her windows in increments of three the entire night. *Tap, tap, tap…tap, tap, tap*…beckoning her to open the window and allow it to enter her room. For six days, it continued to tap on her windows, and she could feel the creature watching her as she walked to and from school. She even skipped school to see a movie at the west end movie theater with a boy from her high school; however, even this public space was not safe from the Lechuza's gaze. "There were a few people in the theater," Angelica recalled, "but it was largely empty. Anyway, I could hear feathers rustle even inside the theater, but my friend didn't hear anything." Ending just as mysteriously as it had started, the knocking on her window stopped at three o'clock in the morning on the sixth day.

This was the event that shaped Angelica both spiritually and philosophically. She had come face-to-face with something completely unexplainable but not all together unexpected. Aside from her aunt's occult activities, Ms. Lopez's grandmother, a curandera of some renown, blamed Angelica for the death of Angelica's father and mother. Was the Lechuza Angelica's transformed grandmother or a demonic messenger summoned to carry out her vengeance? Or is the Lechuza something else entirely?

Researcher Jon Gonzalez received the following account from Robert Bocanegra:

> *Myself and a few cousins of mine had a night out drinking and were on our way to my cousin's house late at night around 3:00–4:00 a.m. As we were driving on the side road by the old St. Cecilia Catholic Church* [only a few hundred yards from Angelica's encounter], *we saw this big --- black thing that looked like a bird flying close to our car. It got close. We all knew it wasn't a bird—it looked more like a gargoyle, its black wings covered its whole body like it was hiding his face while our lights beamed on his whole body. We, all macho dudes including myself, were all frightened, and the only thing we said was, "You saw that right?"*

Regardless of what this creature is, perhaps the better question is why, if the Lechuza is a new and regional myth, does the creature's description sound so very familiar?

Throughout history, the idea of witches either controlling giant supernatural owl creatures or transforming into them has been quite common, but none are as famous as the harpies of Greek mythology. There are many versions of the story of Jason and the Argonauts, but all include an encounter with Phineus of Salmydessus, a king tormented by the harpies as a punishment from Zeus. In some versions, the harpies are killed, and in others, their lives are spared after they promise to leave Phineus alone. Some versions regard them as manifestations of storms, while others considered them monstrous creatures akin to centaurs, gorgons or hundred-armed giants. The harpies earned the nickname the "Hounds of Zeus" for their actions and as guardians of the underworld. But the most important description of the harpies comes to us from the ancient Greek poet Virgil in his work the *Aeneid*: "Bird-bodied, girl-faced things they are; abominable their droppings, their hands are talons, their faces haggard with hunger insatiable."

While the harpy would remain popular throughout the Middle Ages in European literature, it does have an even more ancient predecessor: the

Burney relief found in Babylon and believed to be carved in the late 1800s BC to the mid-1700s BC. *Illustration by author.*

Mesopotamian Lilith. While the idea of Lilith being the first wife of Adam is a more recent interpretation of the creature (if one can consider something from the fifteenth century recent), her mythology is extremely ancient. To the Sumerians and Mesopotamians, Lilith was a night demon (or group of night demons) that was often associated with owls.

While some archaeologists and antiquarians, like Emil Kraeling, believe the famous Burney Relief to be a depiction of Lilith, many modern scholars disagree and associate the figure with the goddess Inanna. But given the way that mythology grows and spreads, it might be that one inspired the other or both grew out of the same cultural milieu. Regardless of the connection, if one even exists, we have yet another depiction of a supernatural creature that appears as a blend of human woman and owl, just as the harpies and Lechuza are described.

But perhaps the most notable aspect of Lilith as an owl demon comes to us from the prophet Isaiah. The English word *Lilith* is a transliteration from the Hebrew word *lilit*, which appears in Isaiah 34:14 (just after the sheydim we discussed earlier). It must be noted that many modern translations do translate *lilit* as "screech owl" or just "owl" because that is what the Hebrew word literally means, but many older translations have used other, more mystical equivalents. Without getting into the weeds on how languages are translated, there are two schools of thought about what the prophet was conveying with his list of "creatures" in Isaiah 34. The more modern versions render these things as unclean animals like goats, jackals and, of course, owls. The older concept was that the prophet wasn't listing animals but rather demonic spirits like dragons (a stand-in for fallen angels), satyrs (a stand-in for demons) and *lamia* (a stand-in for female night demons).

Lamia is a Latin word that means "vampire" but not in the way we imagine. The myth of Lamia comes from the Greeks, and in at least one version, she was a Libyan queen whose children were murdered by Hera after the vengeful (and rather petty) goddess learned of the queen's affair with Zeus. Zeus turned Lamia into a monster so that she could exact her vengeance on the children of other human mothers. (This doesn't seem very productive, but OK.) While often conceptualized as a sea monster since her father was Poseidon, Lamia was believed to haunt the night as a demon and consume children. There are some accounts that call her the queen of the Laestrygonians, a tribe of giant cannibals who make an appearance in Homer's epic poem the *Odyssey*. It must be noted that while seen as an individual, Lamia could be pluralized and was often used to describe groups of vampiric beings.

Bridges and Paranormal Entities

If I may be conversational for a moment, I love learning about how sightings of Sasquatch (whatever they may be) intertwine, merge and change D/FW mythology and folklore. It's clean, fun (for me at least) and entirely academic, but encounters of the White Rock Lake goatman and Ms. Lopez's Lechuza beg us to dig just a little deeper than many find comfortable. To explore these topics, we need to leave the realm of sociology and look into the world of the paranormal. Just as folklore and urban legends are often used to convey messages about society or give direction to the younger generation, they can also emerge as explanations for paranormal encounters. Sometimes, these stories are used to make sense of phenomena that make no sense—phenomena that are so far removed from our common lives that they make us question our own sanity.

We've all heard the stories of trolls hiding under bridges in Norwegian folklore—not to mention the bridges that have been ascribed to Satan's handiwork. (There are numerous devil's bridges littered across Europe.) River crossings and crossroads are often seen as places with high paranormal potential in ancient religions and traditions. This is even reflected in the story of the Headless Horseman and Ichabod Crane. In the story, the headless phantom couldn't cross the bridge that Mr. Crane uses to escape because it was built over a river. It may seem preposterous at first, but given all of the ancient folklore associated with bridges and the number of modern paranormal researchers who have captured ghostly apparitions on their cameras, unknown voices on EVP recordings and even physical assaults from unseen forces, can it be rejected outright?

Nearly all of the goatmen stories in the D/FW area (and many beyond Texas, for that matter) occur near bridges and graveyards—places that have been dubbed liminal zones by author Merrily Harpur in her 2006 book *Mystery Big Cats*. These liminal zones, Ms. Harpur writes, "are the transitional zones between one area and another—the kind of no-man's-land traditionally regarded as magical."

This is notable, as researcher Nick Redfern also connects bridges and paranormal phenomena in a 2013 article on the Old Alton Bridge goatman:

> *Bridges, as anyone with even the most basic knowledge of Forteana will be aware, have been directly linked with paranormal phenomena for years; in fact, for centuries, no less....And, of course, there is the world's most famous winged humanoid, Mothman, and the tragic events of December 1967, involving the huge Silver Bridge at Point Pleasant, West Virginia that collapsed into the dark depths of the Ohio River, drowning dozens. Is it simply a mere coincidence that old bridges and bizarre entities go together, in definitive hand in glove style? No, just maybe it is not.*

Not only should these connections not be rejected, but the common theme of the areas being frequented by occultists should also be considered. Is it possible that the cow skull mask–wearing satanists of Old Foamy Road aren't just local hokum? While the story is almost certainly false, it isn't out of the question that it was inspired by something real or that those who practice pagan rituals would use these isolated and wild places for their worship. It is here that I need to tell of my own explorations in the D/FW area.

One does not have to travel far to find abandoned houses, old silos or large storm drains with pentagrams and animal debris. Much of this is just the result of teenagers trying to be edgy, but in my career in the real estate title industry, I have personally seen several cases in the D/FW area of foreclosed homes being broken into and used for magical practices that include the sacrifice of animals. It may sound strange that there are active occultists in the Bible Belt, but it certainly does exist and has for quite some time.

Given the history of conflict between occult pagan practitioners and the Christian Church in the West, not to mention the United States specifically, the idea that those who followed pre-Christian religions would meet in secret or isolated locations is not just possible, but it is also probable. In the same way that Christians in Japan would disguise their religious artifacts as statues used in Buddhism or even Taoist practices, many occultists and

A Templar Knight and Baphomet. *Illustration by the author.*

neo-pagans hid their practices until very recently. This practice might even trace back to the infamous Templar Knights.

The Templar Knights were officially disbanded under the order of Pope Clement V in AD 1312 for charges of heresy. The popular theory is that the order had adopted Islamic traditions, practices and beliefs and that the name "Baphomet" (the demon that the Templars supposedly worshipped) is an Old French corruption of the name Muhammed. Some historians disagree and argue that Baphomet is a coded message connected to alchemy, and others claim that it is simply the proper name for the devil. While there is no consensus about where this Baphomet figure comes from, what we know for certain is that by the nineteenth century, Baphomet was believed to be a demon and was drawn as a *sheydim/shedim* (Hebrew word for "goat-shaped demon") by occultists. His image has been popularized by modern neo-paganists and Satanists in movies, television programs and even statues displayed outside of state capitols as protests of monuments dedicated to the Ten Commandments.

The Templars were destroyed on a bloody Friday the thirteenth in 1312, which is why Friday the thirteenth is considered unlucky to this day. If the

Templar Knights were secret occultists, as was claimed, and members did escape the bloody purge, it is possible that this order continues on in smaller, fragmented occult covens that maintain a tradition with a Christian exterior but Satanist interior. Now, what does any of this have to do with paranormal entities like the Lechuza or the goatman of White Rock Lake? To untie this Gordian knot, we'll discuss what Nick Redfern and other researchers have named "tulpas" and the idea of thought forms.

Theory 1: The Tulpa Theory

You can be forgiven for not knowing what a tulpa, is as it is derived from Tibetan mysticism and was popularized in the twentieth century by numerous spiritualists, like Alexandra David-Néel, William Walker Atkinson and Annie Besant. The word *tulpa* means "manifestation or emanation of thought," which is why many authors, like John Keel and Nick Redfern, often use the term "thought form" to describe the concept. Essentially, a tulpa is a manifestation of collective belief born of the "energy of human thought." These creatures are not mere puppets, though. Often believed to have their own personalities and agendas, tulpas are simply created by the power of the collective belief and not controlled by it. However, some would note that the tulpa is not completely divorced from the power of changing views and may grow or evolve just as the legend or myth grows and evolves.

Thus the odd paranormal phenomenon found at the Old Alton Bridge and the appearances of the goatman at White Rock Lake could be the result of people's collective beliefs, specifically the worship of Baphomet by neo-pagans (if they indeed exist) or even the collective imaginations of those interested in the goatman legend in general. A similar but inversed proposition is presented by fellow researcher and Messianic pastor Bruce Tentzer.

Theory 2: The Demon Hypothesis

Pastor Tentzer suggested that the paranormal entities found at these locations (whether they were drawn there by occult practices or are native to these areas) existed long before these stories and it is actively manipulating human mythology and occult behavior to feed them and give them power in some way. In ages past, these creatures were worshipped as gods by people coming to certain locations and using icons of what they looked like (horned humanoids), but now people are going out and giving them attention by researching them and making television shows or movies about them. Perhaps these things are going out of their way to keep the idea of goatmen in the regional vocabulary because the attention it brings serves the same purpose as worship did in the past.

Pastor Tentzer even points to the consistent examples of supernatural goatmen like Pan, Leshy, the satyrs and the sheydim as evidence that these hybrid forms might actually be their natural appearance. Is it possible that the sheydim that haunted the ancient Israelites have followed humanity across the world and are just changing their sales pitch to match the new and changing times?

Mountain Creek Monster

Bigfoot of Grand Prairie and the Best Southwest Cities

When looking for Bigfoot in Dallas, Texas, there are two areas to investigate. The first is the wide expanse of the Trinity River bottoms east of I-45 around the Hutchins border. Due to seasonal flooding, environmental concerns and a lack of development, this area is quite wild when compared to regions to the north and west of Dallas. So, it isn't surprising that there are some researchers who have made claims of filming Bigfoot in those areas. What might be even more interesting are the sightings that come from the Mountain Creek area on Dallas's southwest side. The Mountain Creek is a tributary of the Trinity that was impounded to create the Mountain Creek Lake and Joe Pool Lake. It runs south from Irving into Dallas and Grand Prairie.

Grand Prairie was founded in 1863 by Alexander McRae Dechman, who actually named the community "Dechman" after himself. He purchased the land to harvest timber and, after failing to establish a homestead, returned after the Civil War to eventually trade half of the property to T&P Railroad. This meant that the rail would go through his property, ensuring the survival of the town he'd helped to found. Though the railroad depot was named Dechman, the first U.S. post office opened in 1877 under the name "Deckman," due to poor penmanship on the application forms. However, apparently no one liked the name because by 1909 the town was incorporated with the new name Grand Prairie.

There are two competing stories as to how Dechman/Deckman became Grand Prairie. The first, and official, is that there was confusion among the post office employees because T&P Railroad maps labeled the area as "the grand prairie," due to a series of earlier surveys from 1850 to 1858 designating the region between Dallas and Fort Worth "the grand prairie of Texas." Supposedly, the U.S. post office just renamed the town, and nobody cared. The second, and far more romantic, version tells of a beautiful young actress touring the area and, on stepping foot on the Dechman depot, declaring, "My, what a grand prairie!" And the rest is history. Whichever way it happened, it's clear that no one was overly fond of the town's original name.

That being said, while the area west of Dallas is basically an open prairie, the area between Grand Prairie and Cedar Hill is not; in fact, it's a green space that runs north to the Trinity and southeast through the Best Southwest cities, as well as Ovilla, Red Oak, Rockett, Midlothian, Waxahachie, Reagor Springs, Ennis, Palmer, Garrett, Crisp, Alsdorf and then to the Trinity River, over forty miles southeast of Dallas. The reason for this is a long limestone escarpment known as the Cedar Ridge. (This is why there are so many Cedar Ridge names all over this area of Dallas.) Most of North Texas is flat with a few rolling hills, but the Cedar Ridge is a line of rising bedrock that runs south along Loop 12, which becomes Spur 408, and the ridge continues south through Midlothian and flattens out around Venus, Texas. This ridge creates the highest point in North Texas, Mount Lebanon in Cedar Hill (the hill the town is named for), on which the local radio and television towers are located. This ridge funnels rain runoff into the valley that was created in eons past by Mountain Creek. The combination of this runoff from the Cedar Ridge and the presence of the Mountain Creek creates a green space that, according to archaeologists S. Alan Skinner and Deborah T. Connors, was home to a rather large Caddo community during the Texas archaic period (2500–1000 BC). The village was located at the base of Mount Lebanon, where Joe Pool Lake is now, and lasted for quite a long time because of productive soil and abundant natural resources.

While the slope is far less profound on the eastern side of the escarpment, it still results in a web of fairly large and interconnected creeks that cut through the limestone bedrock—many that even reach the Trinity River. It was this strange topographical phenomenon that attracted most people to this area initially, as the easy access to water along all of these sizable creeks made agriculture extremely productive.

Fun fact: Even with locals, if you ask about the Mountain Creek area, you'll get a blank look. But if you mention the Grand Prairie I-20 Dip (or hill), they'll know what you're referring to. Where Dallas, Grand Prairie,

Cedar Hill and Duncanville all come together around Interstate 20 (just west of Spur 408), the highway crosses the Cedar Ridge escarpment and has to dip down to the prairie below. This is perhaps the most significant incline/decline in Dallas County. On the east side, coming in from Grand Prairie and going into Dallas/Duncanville, you'll notice that there is a large open green space between the westward and eastward lanes. For decades, there was a series of large stones in the shape of Texas that was a local attraction during bluebonnet season. Sadly, it was eventually removed, as it was deemed too distracting for drivers and therefore a hazard.

West Fork Trinity River

South Walton Walker Boulevard, Irving

On a bright August morning in 2011, Rachel Mijares, her husband and several friends were headed out of town for the weekend, when she saw something she couldn't believe. They were going south out of Irving, which was founded in 1903 by Otis Brown and J.O. "Otto" Schulze and named for author Washington Irving ("Rip Van Winkle" and "The Legend of Sleepy Hollow"). Unlike the earlier established towns south of Dallas, which were created around the growing and cultivation of agricultural products, Irving was established with a processing and manufacturing mindset. It started with a blacksmith and two cotton gins but, by the mid-1960s, would boast numerous manufacturing plants, including the largest Frito-Lay plant built at that time, as well as the University of Dallas. Texas Stadium, home to the Dallas Cowboys for thirty-eight seasons, was completed by 1971, only to be torn down in 2010, after the Cowboys moved to Arlington in 2008.

Rachel and her compatriots passed the empty plain where the demolished stadium once stood as they traveled south on Loop 12 (South Walton Walker Boulevard) that morning. As the group crossed the West Fork of the Trinity River, Rachel noticed a large ape-like creature crouching and drinking from the river. "It wasn't all that far away from me," Rachel recalled. "I couldn't see all the fine detail, but it looked like an ape, but much, much bigger. It was bulky, massive really, and very hairy."

When the creature was out of sight of the speeding car, she turned to address the other passengers and ask if they'd seen this oddity as well but stopped herself. "I just kept thinking that there's no way I saw that. We're in

Dallas Demons, Fort Worth Goatmen & Other Terrors of the Trinity River

The creature as described by Mrs. Mijares. *Illustration by the author.*

Dallas—this can't be real. And if I tell these guys, they'll think I'm crazy!" Like so many people do, Rachel kept the event to herself and went on with her life for fear of what other people would say about her sighting.

Fox Hollow Park, Dallas

Rachel's sighting is extremely informative when placed in the context of the next few sightings. You see, she observed the creature near the conjunction of the West Fork of the Trinity River and the Mountain Creek, which flows south into Cedar Hill and Midlothian. As mentioned earlier, the creek was impounded at two junctures to create the Mountain Creek Lake and the significantly larger Joe Pool Lake. Not only is there a green wall around the Mountain Creek as it heads south from the Trinity, but between the two lakes is also a significant and continuous green space that connects to Fish Creek Preserve, the Boy Scouts' Camp Wisdom, Cedar Hill State Park, Fox Hollow Park and innumerable undeveloped green spaces.

It is in this narrow web of wilderness, about eleven miles south of and four years after Rachel's chance observation, that young Leondre Smith was awakened by his loyal pet. It was the middle of the night, and Mr. Smith was made keenly aware that he needed to let his dog out into the backyard if he wanted to avoid cleaning the carpet. He walked downstairs and opened the door, when his dog began acting strangely.

> *It was weird, right. First, he needs to go outside and use the restroom, and as soon as I open the door, he freaks out. So, I turn on the back lights, thinking that maybe he sees a bobcat or something because our backyard is right up on the creek and we don't have a big wooden fence but like this short metal railing that comes up to your waist. I figured whatever it was he was scared at would run away, but when I did, I saw these bright red eyes looking at me. Whatever this thing was, it was really big and walking beside the creek behind my house. There were some lights on in the yard on the other side of the creek, so I could see like an outline of the thing right, and it looked like a swol football player or something, but I could tell it was like way taller than a person cause of where the eyes were. Like this thing was big, and it was looking at me, and I'm thinking, I'm gonna die, but then it just walked off.*

Depiction of Leondre's encounter. *Illustration by the author.*

Leondre's sighting occurred in 2015, and according to reports taken by the Bigfoot Field Researchers Organization (founded in 1995), the following year, a Bigfoot was observed temporarily leaving the shelter of the green wall surrounding the Fish Creek Preserve around dusk. The creature was reportedly seen on several occasions by this same witness, and the sound of several vocalizations and wood knocks were heard. (Wood knocking is believed to be a form of communication.) A police officer speaking to me under the promise of anonymity told of reports of odd howls or screams heard periodically from this area, which is only two miles northwest of Leondre's encounter. Moreover, the Fox Hollow area itself is only a few miles north of Bobby Grashel and the Hallses' encounters some forty-six years earlier.

Initially, this location seems counterintuitive as a favorite spot for a Sasquatch to frequent. After all, I-20 is one of the busiest highways in Texas, the Potter's House (a popular megachurch) and Dallas Baptist University are just up the road (Mountain Creek Parkway) from there and I spent many teenage evenings with friends going to the two movie theaters and surrounding restaurants less than a mile from the Fish Creek Preserve. But the green wall here is deceptively thick and hides a swamp where any Bigfoot migrating from East Texas could feel at home.

The Goatman of Mount Lebanon Road

Cedar Hill

Following the tracks of the Mountain Creek monster south, we run into another series of goatman urban legends, but unlike the other Dallas-area goatman mythology, the goatman of Mount Lebanon Road didn't simply replace or merge with a figure from a previous ghost story or cautionary legend. Instead, this capricious caprinae has its own unique mythology that reflects a much older tradition. It includes a Santa Claus who is way more hardcore than the one Bing Crosby sang about.

As a native to the South Dallas region, I grew up with all of the stories in this book, and in many ways, as a Dallasite, these stories are as much a part of me as anything else. But the goatman of Mount Lebanon Road is a myth that really hits home, as it was part of my childhood. I grew up in nearby DeSoto, so Joe Pool Lake (west of Witch Mountain) and Ellen's Fairway (east of Witch Mountain and just north of Mount Lebanon Road) were integral parts of my youth. Aside from my own encounter, none of the other accounts, stories or mythologies hit home for me the way the goatman of Mount Lebanon Road does.

Founded in 1846, Cedar Hill was one of the largest settlements in the area at the time and was composed of just over 180 unwed men and nearly two hundred families who left the Peters Colony in what is now Denton, Texas. Though a tornado destroyed all but two buildings and killed a number of heads of cattle, a decade later, in April 1856, the town of Cedar Hill persevered and continued to thrive. For most people in the D/FW area, Cedar Hill is known for being the location of the majority of the television and radio antennae that serve all of North Texas and parts of southern Oklahoma. The reason for the cluster is that Mount Lebanon is the highest point in North Texas.

Okay, "mountain" is a bit too strong, but I imagine trekking up it on foot before there were roads and nice neat little paths was no fun. Plus, when you're looking at the tallest hill for hundreds of square miles and you're in a horse-drawn buggy, I think we can forgive you naming it a mountain. Currently home to the scenic eighty-two-acre Lester Lorch Park and a sprawling community of very high-end homes, Mount Lebanon also holds not just Pleasant Valley Cemetery, the oldest cemetery in Cedar Hill, but also a long history of occult and paranormal activity.

Dubbed Ghost Mountain by some of the older inhabitants and Witch Mountain by those coming of age in the late 1980s or so, Mount Lebanon is central to nearly every scary story this once-small town has. The earliest account of paranormal phenomena goes back to before the turn of the previous century, when a man whose name has not been recorded took his favorite coon dogs hunting one evening. After he turned them loose, the beloved animals disappeared into the night and never returned. If this doesn't seem strange to you because your own dog runs off all the time, let me give you some background. Coon dogs are trained to hunt and tree raccoons for their owner, who then shoots the animal. These dogs are well trained and enjoy doing this—they do not simply run off and abandon their masters. Devastated by the loss of the dogs, the man returned to the area for years, only to hear the ghostly howls of his dogs in the distance. There are two other ghostly tales in the area that seem awfully universal—the headless rider and the hanging tree.

The story of the headless rider is Cedar Hill's equivalent of Washington Irving's "The Legend of Sleepy Hollow." The story often told on

Pleasant Valley Cemetery, Cedar Hill. *Courtesy of author.*

Halloween by teenagers looking to scare each other is one of a man who is decapitated after dropping off his daughter at a Halloween party. His body was found next to his horse and buggy on Strauss Road near the corner of Wintergreen and Clark. (This section of Strauss no longer exists.) Every year the headless rider prowls the streets of Cedar Hill looking for a head to replace the one he lost a century ago.

The story of the hanging tree is just the classic story of the hook man, without the hook man. I know that sounds strange, but let me explain. In the classic story of the hook man, a young couple is necking under an oak tree on a little-used road. There is a radio broadcast alerting the community to the escape of a serial killer with a hook for a hand. At some point, the boyfriend gets out of the car and disappears, leaving the girl alone and frightened. As the night goes on, she begins to hear a scratching sound on the roof, which she believes to be the killer's hook. As the dawn comes, a local sheriff arrives and asks the girl to get into his squad car but not to look back, which she of course does. To her horror, she sees that the killer has killed her boyfriend and hung him by his feet from the tree they had parked under. The scratching sound she heard was his fingernails scraping across the top of his car.

A more recent story (which has become popular on ghost story websites and travelogues) is the disappearing cabin of Witch Mountain. The story goes that hikers exploring Witch Mountain (Lester Lorch Park is really the only place left for that) encounter a young barefoot girl. Obviously, fearing the child to be lost, the hapless visitors follow the child to a cabin in a clearing that supernaturally appears. Those poor lost souls who enter the cabin are said to never be seen again.

As an aside, I grew up in nearby DeSoto, and there was an old abandoned cabin near Ten Mile Creek that was supposedly haunted. Stepping inside the cabin meant certain doom for stirring up the evil spirit that inhabited the location. I suppose the moral of both of these stories is to stay away from old abandoned cabins in south Dallas. Generally, this seems like good advice, regardless of malevolent supernatural entities, as tetanus is no joke.

But what does any of this have to do with the goatman of Mount Lebanon Road? A great deal, actually, but let's start at the beginning—way back in the fall of 1969. As previously discussed, Cedar Hill residents had just completed the summer of the Lake Worth Monster, also known as the Greer Island goatman, and a respected firefighter and local couple announced that it had moved into the wilderness area around Mount Lebanon. Remember, the goatman was initially described as a satyr by Jim Marrs of the *Fort Worth Star Telegram*. It is this image of a human-goat hybrid that inspires a new series of tales that entirely replaces the previous ghost stories.

Ghost Mountain becomes Witch Mountain, and the Greer Island goatman evolves into the goatman of Mount Lebanon Road (for Cedar Hill anyway), a paranormal sheydim conjured by "witches" practicing their "forbidden dark arts" on "old Indian burial grounds" or at the Pleasant Valley Cemetery. The story ends up replacing these older legends, as the children in the schoolyards now have this famous monster that is confirmed to live in the area. The new tale, passed on schoolyards and parks by upperclassmen to the younger children and junior high students, was that this sinister satyr had been summoned to hunt for misbehaving children and adolescents.

For Raymond Perez, who grew up in nearby DeSoto, it was his older sisters who warned him of traveling the road at night. According to Mr. Perez's sisters, not only had this frightening hoofed villain been seen frequently by those teenagers looking for a little alone time around Witch Mountain (thirty years ago, the area around Old Plume Road was much quieter and far less inhabited), but several seniors also had a close encounter after their prom night:

> *It was the mid-80s, and these DeSoto High School seniors were headed down to a bonfire at Joe Pool Lake, and they decided to use Mount Lebanon Road as a shortcut since they had the liquor. As they get past Highway 67 and get near Lester Loarch Park, they see this weird creature in the road. It's half man, half goat and almost eight feet tall, and they are going way too fast to stop in time, but this thing jumps on the hood of the truck and is looking into the cab like it's not happy, when the guy driving freaks out and slams into an old oak tree without even hitting the brakes. Surprisingly, the*

Mount Lebanon Road and Lester Loarch Park. *Courtesy of author.*

>*kids, even the two in the truck bed holding the beer and drinks, survived but were all torn up. What freaked out the cops that found them were the hoof prints on the truck's hood and roof.*

While the story clearly follows a fairly well-established pattern for popular folklore, the moral is what provides the key to interpreting this story. Obviously, the intended takeaway from the tale is that teenagers should not be out misbehaving at night (and definitely obey the speed limit; even now, Mount Lebanon Road is not one that you want to be speeding on, particularly at night) because otherwise you'll run into the nightmarish creature lurking in the shadows. It is this aspect of Mount Lebanon's goatman that directly connects him to DeSoto's Hinkey Man of Ten Mile Creek and to Krampus, Santa Claus's dark assistant.

The Hinkey Man of Ten Mile Creek

DeSoto, Dallas

Named after Dr. Thomas Hernando DeSoto Stewart, the city of DeSoto was initially settled in 1847 (making it one of the earliest communities in the area), and the U.S. post office was established in 1888. DeSoto was initially home to a cotton gin, one general store and a surprising number of pecan farms, due to the odd collection of creeks in the area that provided unusually deep soil. Aside from the city's agricultural abundance, Hampton Road would ultimately prove to be the key to DeSoto's early survival. Though the small town really didn't begin to grow until the 1970s and 1980s (there were only about 6,500 people in the 1960s), it was able to survive its population collapsing to around 50 people at the turn of the twentieth century because it was logistically important for settlements farther south.

The Ten Mile Creek is a rather deep and wide tributary of the Trinity River that runs for (wait for it) ten miles. Since going around the creek was a hardship for those on horseback, safe crossings were paramount for travel and trade. No location proved safer than what is now Hampton Road, DeSoto's main street. This topographic advantage funneled business down Hampton, as it became the primary road into Dallas, which allowed DeSoto to grow and prosper until the development of the highway system. But according to Angie Greene, the true menace of the Ten Mile Creek isn't its role as an obstacle but its role as the home to the Hinkey Man.

During her tenure at DeSoto High School, Angie heard tales of the Hinkey Man, in which he was described as a "hairy vagrant with a large fur coat and a limp that walked up and down the Ten Mile Creek in search of children going down into the creek to drink and smoke." The thematic similarities between the Hinkey Man and Cedar Hill's goatman are obvious here, but there are significant differences that connect it to Krampus, a much older mythological figure, and reveal yet another example of how cultural influences impact urban legends that are inspired by contact with the local Bigfoot population.

You may have heard of Krampus recently, as he's appeared in several Christmas-themed horror films (not a sentence one often gets to type), but traditionally he's regarded as Saint Nicholas's aide. While the British version of Santa Claus (the one made famous in Coca-Cola advertising) brings coal to misbehaving children, the eastern European version sends Krampus to kidnap and then beat them (this version of Saint Nick rolls hardcore). And how is Krampus envisioned? A dark, hairy satyr with long horns—a goatman.

Ten Mile Creek. *Courtesy of author.*

Krampus came to Texas through a large influx of Germanic and other eastern European groups who immigrated to Texas in the 1840s and set up certain towns, like New Braunfels, or established smaller communities in other settlements, like in West, Texas. (If you spend any time at all in southern Dallas, you'll discover our love of kolaches and no doubt hear of a certain Czechoslovakian bakery located in that small town.) It is from these tasty pastry–bearing immigrants that Krampus crossed the pond and was delivered to the shores of the Trinity River. (Note: A kolache is a semisweet pastry that surrounds a preserved fruit center and a *klobásník* is a savory version filled with sausage and cheese (but has recently grown to include many other variations like ham, eggs and jalapeno). Interestingly, the klobásník was invented in Texas by Czech immigrants as a savory version of a kolache, yet we all still call klobásníks "kolaches.")

Just as the Red Oak and Reagor Springs Bigfoot became the "Monster," and in Cedar Hill, it became "goatman," for those of eastern European descent in DeSoto, the Bigfoot traversing Ten Mile Creek became the "Hinkey Man."

Depiction of Krampus. *Illustration by the author.*

The Goatman of Shiloh Cemetery, Ovilla and Red Oak

Not content to haunt only Mount Lebanon Road, the goatman is said to frequent Shiloh Cemetery in the nearby city of Ovilla. This still small town was created by early Peters colonists as a fortified settlement, and though it has always been occupied, the railroad bypassing it limited the town's potential growth until the post-1970s Dallas boom. Located six miles from Witch Mountain, and under the loving care of the Shiloh Cumberland Presbyterian Church, Shiloh Cemetery was established around the same time as Cedar Hill's Pleasant Valley Cemetery and is directly connected to it by the same road. It doesn't quite appear that way now due to additions and name changes, but Pleasant Valley is off Texas Plume Road, which ends at Mount Lebanon Road and turns into Tar Road and then Shiloh Road.

Shiloh Cemetery is located less than four thousand feet from Red Oak Creek (originally named Possum Trot), which, you've no doubt guessed, is a tributary of the Trinity River. Since the stories of the goatman of Shiloh Cemetery include red eyes shining from behind the tree line and

Shiloh Cemetery. *Courtesy of author.*

rocks or tree branches being thrown at visitors, it would be safe to suggest that this figure was inspired by a Sasquatch encounter that, like Cedar Hill's version, embraced the Greer Island–inspired goatman moniker. Like Old Alton Bridge, there are no modern stories of people encountering the goatman, but there are plenty of claims of ghostly apparitions appearing on nighttime photographs and visitors being assaulted by spectral or invisible entities.

Note: Ovilla is the birthplace of famed musician Lecil Travis Martin, better known by his stage name, Boxcar Willie. In honor of Mr. Martin, the Ovilla Road (FM 664) overpass at I-35 East is named after his stage persona.

The Cedar Hill Chupacabras

Given that the southern Dallas and Ellis County goatmen and the Hinkey Man are all just localized names for the Mountain Creek Monster (and possibly its family), it's important to see their sightings as part of a series of interconnected phenomena and not just separate events. That being said, Cedar Hill's goatman does have one thing that separates it from the other Mountain Creek Monster encounters and connects it with the White Rock Lake goatman: people see something here that is decidedly not a Bigfoot from time to time.

Perhaps the best account of this was collected by researcher Jon Gonzalez from a man called Shawn, who related the following accounts from his time living in Cedar Hill. His family had recently moved from Missouri, and life was normal for them for several years. His younger sister, scared of the dark, would often drift off to sleep looking at the lights on the radio antennae located on Witch Mountain. One night, though, he noticed his sister glued to the window but looking down and not out at the towers. "What are you looking at?" he asked, but she didn't respond, as if what she was looking at had paralyzed her.

He moved to the window just as the creature she was looking at took off down the alleyway, but what Shawn did see was a shadow of something that appeared to be moving so smoothly that it seemed to float instead of run. Because his neighbor's flood lights were so bright, he could tell that the shadow was unusual, but that was all. The next morning, Shawn spoke with his sister, who described the creature as having large eyes, fangs and something coming out of its mouth.

Depiction of the "thing" on Shawn's bed. *Illustration by the author.*

After looking at a book with a drawing of a purported Chupacabra, he noticed how similar the depiction of the mythical creature was to his sister's description of the thing she saw out of her window that evening. Particularly striking was the proboscis-like tongue included in the image.

Over the next few months, the family experienced other paranormal phenomena, like his sister's (tube not digital) television having repeating text appear on her screen with the simple message, "Shawn did it." The strangeness continued for several months, until one evening when Shawn saw his sister frozen at the top of the stairs staring into his room. He could tell from the expression on her face that she was looking at something that unnerved her, so he called out to her. She replied, "I don't know but this thing with big black eyes was standing on your bed and then when it heard you, it sunk down and disappeared."

The final direct encounter with an unknown entity while Shawn lived in Cedar Hill occurred just a few months later in the early spring, when the windows could be kept open for a breeze. While walking down the stairs around midday, he noticed a pair of legs in the backyard. The angle he was at prevented him from seeing more of the creature, but he saw what appeared to be large, hulking hairless kangaroo or dog's feet. By the time he ran down the stairs to look into the backyard, the creature had gone and was nowhere to be seen. The phenomena ended after that, and to this day, neither he nor his family has seen anything similar. The other paranormal strangeness also ended, making us question whether the creatures seen by Shawn's sister were one and the same or different entities drawn for the same reason.

Note: The lore surrounding the chupacabra (pronounced *choo-pah-cah-brah*) is complicated by the fact that, like Dallas's goatman, it became a catch-all title for many different unknown animals and paranormal creatures. Initially, *el chupacabras* was depicted as a small reptilian alien with spines and large eyes, similar to what Shawn's sister described. But despite the original renderings and later alternatives that involved wings or even humanoid appearances, if you type "chupacabra" in your search engine today, you'll find endless streams of pictures showing a unique breed of canine dubbed "Blue Dogs" by researchers Ken Gerhard and Jeff Stewart. This strange hairless breed of coyote and domesticated dog seems to have developed naturally. Somehow, the population was isolated long enough that the inbreeding allowed certain deformities to become standard traits, which is why they appear so odd. That being said, the primary feature of a chupacabra is the desiccation (draining the blood) of farm animals to supposedly feed like a vampire, and the Blue Dogs seem incapable of this feat, indicating that the real culprit, the real chupacabra, has not been identified.

The Ten Mile Creek

DeSoto

While the lack of modern sightings in some of these creeks may give the impression that the local Sasquatch populations have stopped frequenting these waterways, I should point out that most people do not disclose their encounters and perhaps the most striking Bigfoot story I have heard comes from the Ten Mile Creek. This unique encounter comes to me from an individual who I know personally. About twelve miles east of the cluster of sightings around Mountain Creek Parkway is the city of Lancaster, Texas. A small suburb of Dallas, Lancaster is positioned between I-35 and I-45. Aside from Bonnie and Clyde robbing the town bank in 1934, there isn't a lot that most people would find interesting in its history. It is a rather pleasant place to live, though, which is why the Knollmans chose to move into a small subdivision right off Belt Line Road and next to the Ten Mile Creek.

It was a normal summer night around 10:00 or 10:30 p.m. in 2013, when April noticed that the normal animal sounds and the constant dog barking had gone quiet. "It was weirdly quiet," she recalled.

> *I mentioned something to my husband about how quiet it was, and though he hadn't noticed it before, he stopped and looked at me and said, "Yeah, you're right. It is unusually quiet." And then like it was planned, we heard this loud howl, and we both froze. We'd never heard anything like it. It was weird, and then, after a few minutes, we heard it again, but this time it sounded like it was right outside. Then a few minutes later, the same howl but farther away, and that's when we realized that this thing was going east*

The Knollman house and map of the surrounding area. *Courtesy of author.*

down the Ten Mile Creek. The first call had been west of our house and probably by quite a bit, given how loud the one right next to our house was, but the third one was farther down but from the other side, so it was going down the creek. We heard one more call much farther down the creek, and so it was a lot quieter.

April had recently become interested in Sasquatch due to several television programs she had begun watching and recognized the howls. She quickly looked through sound files online and found several purported recordings from the Pacific Northwest that were identical to what they had heard. Her husband, who was far less convinced of the hairy hominid's existence, admitted that the recordings matched the sound that they had heard that fateful evening. Moreover, April revealed that while on a family walk only a few days before, they had encountered a strong stench of sulfur. (The Florida Bigfoot has been dubbed the "skunk ape" due to its famous odor.) While relating these very recent events to me (the howls had occurred only two days earlier), a look of sheer horror came upon April's face.

It was only during our conversation that she remembered an event from two years before on a bright, pleasant spring morning. It was around 10:30 or 11:00 a.m., and their youngest child was out playing in the backyard. The yard is fenced in with a six-foot-high wooden privacy fence, and the kitchen has an excellent view of the modest-sized area, so there was no way for a five-year-old to get into trouble. April had been working in the kitchen and could hear him playing and singing to himself, when suddenly the sounds shifted to a cry of utter terror. She rushed out, fearing something terrible had occurred, and was frantically checking the child for what certainly had to be a life-threatening injury.

The monster, as described by the Knollman boy. *Illustration by the author.*

Thankfully, she found no wound, and she tried to comfort the child for nearly half an hour before he was composed enough to relate the events that had so traumatized him. He told her a story of playing with his toys and looking up to see a "hairy monster" looking at him over the fence. He said that he could see the monster's shoulders and head over the fence and that it had both hands resting on the top of the fence. The small child was stunned by the sight, but it wasn't until it opened its mouth to smile at him that he saw the large canine teeth (obviously not his words). At the time, April had chalked up the entire episode to perhaps the child falling asleep and having a nightmare, though she thought it was odd, since she could hear him playing and singing to himself. She now realized that his hairy monster had been real—and watching her child.

But it isn't just Sasquatch that the Ten Mile Creek seems to hold.

The Ten Mile Creek Pterosaur

It was a normal June morning in 1992. A friend and I had spent the day fishing in the Ten Mile Creek. The creek winds through Duncanville, DeSoto, Lancaster and Hutchins like a drunken snake and cuts deeply through the limestone bedrock. It's between fifteen and twenty feet wide in most places, and the walls of the creek can reach as high as thirty or forty feet. Due to the high limestone sides and dense green wall, the creek is inaccessible, except for those places where the side walls collapsed, creating a ramp of rock and earth. It was around 11:00 a.m., and what fish there were had stopped biting. My friend was already packed and up the walkway. I had just reached the tree line when I heard a sound I'd never heard before or since.

It sounded like the caw of a crow but louder and uglier—if that makes any sense. It startled me, so I stopped and poked my head out from behind the tree line. At first, I thought I was looking at the largest blue heron I had ever seen. It was the right shape and color overall, but when it passed in front of me and the wingtip was less than five feet from my face, I realized that this "blue heron" had no feathers—just skin. It was at this time that I noticed that what I thought were its legs sticking out behind it was actually a long-flanged tail. I was able to watch it for another five or ten seconds as it sailed down the creek and then banked right and continued to follow the creek away from me.

Just as it disappeared, my friend hollered down at me, "You coming or what?"

I responded, "Did you just see that pterodactyl that just flew by?" He laughed, said I was crazy and then headed home, telling me to catch up or he'd eat the sandwiches before I got there. I spent the next twenty-plus years convincing myself that I hadn't seen a pterodactyl but rather a blue heron and that I was wrong about the entire experience. It took time, but I finally came to realize that not only was I not alone in seeing living pterodactyls in general, but my sighting was not unique in the D/FW area. It wasn't even unique in the Ten Mile Creek.

Ten Mile Pterosaur the Sequel

It was a clear and beautiful Sunday in March when Christine Daniels and her teenage daughter, Rose, had their encounter.

My daughter was going to spend her spring break with her father, so I was taking her to DFW airport. We live in Italy, so the fastest way to get there at the time [2014] was to go north on I-35 and then go west on I-20. The flight was at one o'clock, and they always tell you to get there three hours early, so we left the house around 9:00 a.m. We were coming into Lancaster around 9:30, when I saw what I thought was a big bird on the right-hand side of the highway, where the grass is between the highway and the frontage road. It just looked like a big dark brown crane or vulture from the back, so I was focusing on the road until Rose shouted, "Mom! Look at that! It's not a bird!"

We were coming right up on it, and so I looked closer and that's when I saw it didn't have feathers. It was smooth like a bat, but it had a long tail. I didn't get that good a look at it because even though it was only like thirty or forty feet away when it was beside us, my daughter was between me and it. So, I didn't get a good look at the front of this thing before we passed it and it followed the frontage road down under the bridge and went into that river that's at Beltline Road [Ten Mile Creek].

Her daughter later described the creature as "like a lizard and a pelican had a baby."

Rose also noted, "I'm not a big fan of dinosaurs but this looked like it was one. It didn't belong in our time." When I asked both women if they had told anyone else of their sighting, Christine said the following: "I didn't tell nobody about it because I didn't think anybody would believe me, and it didn't seem to matter."

The location (35E and Beltline) where the creature flew back into the Ten Mile Creek. *Courtesy of author.*

The Winged Weirdo of Witch Mountain

College student Daniel Mentz lives and works on either side of Cedar Hill's Witch Mountain. This means that much of his time is spent in or around the dense green space by Joe Pool Lake and Cedar Hill State Park that is home to the Mountain Creek Monster, yet his encounters were a bit different from the rest. "The first time I saw it, I was coming home from working the early-morning shift, so it's like 10:30 a.m., and I'm going west on FM 1382 toward Sleepy Hollow Road. I'm right going through where the road was cut into the limestone hill, and I see it glide right in front of me and disappear into the tree line."

What caught Daniel's attention was the long tail and strange color of the creature in front of him:

> *It was right in front of me for a while before it went left and went into the trees. It wasn't too big, like maybe a five-or-six-foot wingspan, but it was sort of a red and had blue on its crest and tail. I thought that was weird, particularly the tail. It was long, like a lizard's, but it had this strange diamond or like a less round kinda egg shape at the end.*
>
> *Second time was like two months later at 8:30 or so. It was a Saturday, and I was going on my normal walk, when I heard all these branches just going nuts behind me. It sounded like something big jumped out of the tree, and so I look up, and this thing flies over my head and lands on the trunk of this other tree in front of me. It is maybe thirty feet off the ground when*

Location of the first sighting. *Courtesy of author.*

Location of the second sighting.
Courtesy of author.

I realize that it's that same strange bird I saw on FM 1382. The thing scurries up the tree like a lizard would and then perches on a branch for a bit before flying off. It was weird because the face was like an iguana—not a bird.

Though smaller—about half the size of the others—the creature Daniel described matches the other four witness descriptions, and when presented with an image of a *Rhamphorhynchoid pterosaur,* he readily pointed to it as the weird bird he observed, just as Alan, Rachel and I have.

Dragons through History

While there is a photograph of a small child holding a *Rhamphorhynchoid pterosaur* that was purportedly published in a Texas newspaper in the 1950s, no researcher has been able to confirm its veracity. So, if we disregard that one image, according to famed researcher Ken Gerhard (noted expert in winged anomalous creatures), the earliest modern accounts of living pterosaurs in Texas date to 1964, around San Antonio. Over the years, Mr. Gerhard has taken more than fifty accounts of living pterosaurs in North America. (Of the accounts above, only my sighting was included in that count at the writing of this book.) While most of the accounts he has collected are of larger (man-sized) pterosaurs seen in northern Mexico, the Rio Grande Valley and along the West Coast, as far north as Alaska, the accounts he has received from the North Texas/southern Oklahoma region exclusively describe a smaller *Rhamphorhynchoid pterosaur*.

"It's really very interesting, accounts of these smaller pterosaurs are remarkably similar; wingspan of eight to ten feet, darker coloration and either a stubby or no crest. While not all accounts include descriptions of tails, when they do, they're almost always described as having a 'diamond' or 'triangularly shaped' flange at the end."

Researcher Joe Taylor of the Mount Blanco Fossil Museum has noted the same commonalities among accounts of living pterosaurs seen in and around Crosbyton, Texas (about five hours west of Dallas). One individual he interviewed claimed to have seen them frequently in his youth, as they would use the updrafts from the ravine next to the farm where he worked to glide. But again, this witness's youth was the 1970s—not the 1930s or late 1800s. So, why don't we have stories of these creatures going further back? Have they somehow been able to remain hidden for the last few centuries? Well, the answer to this might actually be yes and no.

THE FORT WORTH FLYER

When one hears tales of dragons, their minds are carried to an age of steel-covered men with great swords and towers of stone in medieval Europe—not to truckers in big rigs on concrete roads in modern-day Fort Worth, Texas. Some researchers, however, claim that dragon myths were born out of conflicts between humanity and small populations of dinosaurs that managed to survive until relatively recently. After all, the word *dinosaur* didn't exist until it was coined by paleontologist Sir Richard Owen in 1841. It would only stand to reason that if some species of dinosaur (and other associated non-dinosaur reptiles such as pterosaurs and mosasaurs) did survive until recent

Re-creation of the purported *Rhamphorhynchoid pterosaur*. *Illustration by the author.*

times, that earlier civilizations would have called these amazing creatures by another name, like dragon. As evidence for this claim, many researchers point to possible sightings of surviving pterosaurs soaring in the skies of North Texas and southern Oklahoma regions, D/FW included.

One recent account of these reclusive reptiles comes courtesy of researcher Kent Hovind, who received a call from a gentleman named Alan, who has been an over-the-road truck driver since 1999. After twenty years in his profession, Alan has developed an appreciation for the local fauna of a given area, so it wasn't unusual for him to take notice of a large, low-flying creature on June 14, 2018. It was a nice clear morning, around 10:30 a.m., when Alan found himself delivering a load of water heaters to a customer between Dallas and Fort Worth. He was heading east on Interstate 30, just outside of the 820 interchange, when he saw what he thought was a large dark brown or reddish-brown pelican gliding south, about twenty feet off the ground. "It was really big," Alan noted. "Biggest pelican I'd ever seen. The wings were like four or five feet long, but I couldn't get a good look at the overall wingspan because it flew in front of me so I could only see the profile. And I thought it was something like a pelican because of the overall shape and how it had its neck curved back like an *S*." As he got closer, though, Alan realized that this "pelican" wasn't a bird at all, but a living pterosaur:

> *I was looking at this thing for about twenty seconds and got really close to it. At first, I thought it was a bird carrying something, but then I realized it was a pterosaur with a long tail that had a diamond-shaped flange at the end. I know the story sounds crazy, but I wasn't more than twenty feet away from this thing when it flew right in front of my truck. Plus, it was late enough in the morning that the light was coming down on it, so it isn't like the sun was in my eyes. The tail, that diamond shape at the end, and the fact that it didn't have any feathers was what I focused on because it was unlike anything I've ever seen. I could clearly see this was a pterodactyl, and I know what it was that I saw.*

Kennedale Rhamphorhynchus

It was a warm summer night as Rachel Urban drove to her home in Kennedale, about eight miles south of Alan's encounter (but a few years earlier). She was headed west on Sublet Drive when a creature flew right over her car and then banked right and disappeared into the night. Mrs. Urban said,

> I was in a residential area, and with so many streetlights, I could have driven it safely without my headlights, plus I was doing just under thirty miles an hour when it passed over me on the driver's side, so I was able to get a good look at it. At first, I saw it out of the corner of my eye, and I thought maybe it was a big owl flying next to my car, but then I turned my head to get a better look, and I couldn't believe what I was looking at. When it was just a bit in front of my car and was in my headlights, the creature turned right, so I could see the head and body even better than when it was next to me. I grew up with brothers who loved dinosaurs, so I knew immediately that it was some kind of pterodactyl, but I still couldn't believe it.

Mrs. Urban described the creature she saw as "having a dull reddish-brown tone to it, almost rust-colored skin—definitely no feathers. When it flew in front of me, I could see that the wing tips were on either side of my car, so the wingspan was about eight or nine feet across. It had a small backwards-facing head crest and a long tail with a triangular thing at the end of it. What was weird was that when it was at my side and in front, it had its neck curved back so it kinda looked like a pelican or a crane."

The Thunderbird

While some have speculated that artwork of the wyvern from medieval Europe is evidence that *Rhamphorhynchoid pterosaurs* were once endemic to the Old World, many more have theorized that pterosaurs are the origins of the Native American deity called Thunderbird. (It has been theorized that the pressures of the extreme changing of the European climate forced these "dragons" to attack livestock for an easy meal, which brought them into conflict with farmers and led to them being hunted to extinction.) But this seems unlikely, as a Thunderbird is usually viewed as exceptionally large, like those found in the Rio Grande Valley that seem to belong to the pteranodontidae family. Often described by pilots as being the size of a Cessna while in flight, confirmation of these creature's size comes from eyewitness Darleen Dhillon:

> *In the early '70s, my husband and I ran a small import store. We became friends with a couple who made frequent trips to Mexico to buy stuff, some of which we carried in our store. When we would visit them at their place of business, our attention would be riveted by a large [unfossilized] pterodactyl skull....They had purchased it on a trip to northern Mexico. As for a description of the skull, I'd say it was about two and a half feet long and maybe one and a half feet high. Since it was about forty-five years ago that I saw it, this is best that I can recall. What stood out, though, was the dominant bony crest on the top of it.*

The theory is that the larger pterosaurs ride the updrafts and wind gusts in front of a thunderstorm. Given their size, strange appearance and association with storms, these relic pteranodontidae became symbolic of the Thunderbird deity. While it is entirely speculative, the real weakness of this theory (even if it is correct) is that it focuses entirely on the much larger pterosaurs found in northern Mexico and South Texas and not the smaller *Rhamphorhynchoid pterosaurs* seen in the North Texas and southern Oklahoma region. (There are also accounts of *Rhamphorhynchoid pterosaurs* in Georgia and other locations across the United States.) So, even if these larger pterosaurs are the inspiration for the Thunderbird, it doesn't explain why we have no legends or stories of the smaller versions seen by denizens of the Dallas/Fort Worth Metroplex.

Living Pterosaurs and Ghost Lights

While the Thunderbird mythology might not have been influenced by the smaller pterosaurs indigenous to the D/FW region, some researchers point to the ubiquitous stories of certain ghost lights as evidence of the presence of rhamphorhynchoids throughout Texas history. It is believed by some researchers looking into the possibility of a surviving species of pterosaurs in Papua New Guinea (locally known as the "ropen") that they have bioluminescent capabilities (the ability to light up like a firefly or certain fish and octopi). The most obvious use of this would be as a mating display, but some have speculated that it could also be useful for hunting. Where the deep-sea angler fish uses its light to attract prey, the pterosaurs could use light displays to attract insects, which then attract bats that the diminutive dragons catch and feed on.

Though no one has actually observed this behavior or has even directly reported a pterodactyl demonstrating bioluminescence, researcher Jon Gonzalez recalled an event from his youth. It occurred one evening while growing up in South Texas's Rio Grande Valley near McAllen (over five hundred miles south of Dallas). "On one occasion I was outside in his [Gonzalez's grandfather] back patio at night when a flock of migrating birds in *V* formation flew overhead. This seemed like a regular thing except on closer inspection, the birds, which appeared to resemble seagulls, seemed to all have shocks coming out of their mouths. It looked like when you are jumping a car, and the positive and negative cables make contact or when you are trying to start a butane lighter. That is what seemed to be coming from their beaks and eyes."

This observation is eerily reminiscent of what has come to be known as the Van Meter Visitor. For several days in 1903, a large, bat-like creature (that many modern researchers render as being very similar to a large pterodactyl) stalked the town of Van Meter before either being killed or driven away. A key element of the story is the description of a horn that could illuminate so brightly that many found it blinding. While the concept of a nocturnal, bioluminescent pterodactyl is preposterous—at first glance—it does go a

Drawing of the Van Meter Visitor and Jon Gonzalez's sighting. *Illustration by the author.*

long way toward explaining the ghost lights so frequently observed in certain regions of Texas. Certainly, the most famous of these ghost lights are found in Marfa, Texas (about four hundred miles outside of the metroplex).

Given that Marfa is part of the Rio Grande Valley and has a similar topography as that area surrounding Crosbyton, it isn't difficult to connect the ghost light phenomenon with the relic pterosaur population. The real question, though, is do we have any other situations where these rhamphorhynchoids overlap with other ghost lights? In fact, there is—at Witch Mountain in Cedar Hill. Before the development of Witch Mountain in Cedar Hill, teens in the '50s and '60s would park on the Grand Prairie side late at night and look for the ghost lights known to frequent the area in the summer. Supporting this idea back in 2014 and 2015, there were several videos captured of purported UFOs flying over Cedar Hill before a thunderstorm. In the video from 2015, two unexplained lights lazily dance across the sky, and the lights would occasionally go out and reappear nearby a few seconds later.

While the video does not give us any clear image of what is being recorded or their true size, we can conclude that the lights in the recordings were not traditional aircraft. Though drones cannot be ruled out entirely, it should be noted that the objects glow only one solid light and lack the other colors commonly found on drones. Moreover, one video includes the objects in front of a thunderstorm, which any drone operator will tell you is careless—at best—given how light civilian drones are. The updrafts alone are likely to carry a drone outside the range of the operator's remote, and winds greater than fifteen miles per hour are usually avoided for the same reason. Given that the low-end average wind speed for a thunderstorm is around thirty miles per hour, it does seem that the drone theory is less likely. An additional observation that goes against the drone option is how the lights move in the video.

Instead of the jerky and seemingly erratic movements of a drone fighting high winds, the luminosities appear to use the storm's updrafts to fly and rely on the wind to keep them aloft in much the same way a vulture would. Coupled with the fact that neither of the videos shows the objects performing any of the physics-defying feats common among most UFO encounters, a biological origin for these unknown aerial illuminations does seem far more likely than one would first assume.

That being said, despite all of these observations and overlaps of observed phenomena, the simple truth is that the videos are inconclusive at best. There is nothing in either video to directly connect the lights to anything specific, much less a surviving population of bioluminescent nocturnal *Rhamphorhynchoid pterosaurs*. And though Mr. Gonzalez's account from his youth is intriguing, we sadly cannot confirm that what he saw was a flock of pterosaurs—much less that they were the kind of *Rhamphorhynchoid pterosaurs* seen in the D/FW area—or even that the relic reptiles in question are bioluminescent.

But perhaps the answer lies in our lack of mythology about these creatures.

Hiding in Plain Sight

Ultimately, in many ways, the lack of stories and myths about the existence of these strange *Rhamphorhynchoid pterosaurs* is itself evidence of how they've managed to survive in the area for so long: we just don't see them. This is not to say that they are invisible or anything like that, but one consistent theme of all the sightings above and others that I've heard is how much like a heron, crane or pelican these creatures look when they fly. I, while only forty feet away from one, thought it nothing more exotic than a large blue heron—a species that is both local and well known. It wasn't until it was immediately in front of me that I recognized it for what it was. How many times has someone caught a glimpse of these creatures and not thought anything of it?

Moreover, if these creatures are indeed nocturnal with a very low—critically endangered—population, as is believed, there is very little reason for most people to ever see one. Add the fact that pterosaurs are not actually dinosaurs but reptiles, and their metabolism wouldn't require them to be out hunting as often as a bird would. Though flight does require a higher calorie count, by being cold-blooded, these soaring reptilians could go for long periods after eating only a few pounds—like a crocodile does. This would mean they only need to hunt for food once or twice a week or even a month.

Their rarity combined with their nocturnal nature and infrequent need to leave their dens is the perfect recipe for these rhamphorhynchoids to go entirely undetected by people. Throw in their superficial similarities to herons, and it is perfectly understandable why these dragons of the D/FW Metroplex have managed to fly under the radar.

Aquatic Anomalies

Most lakes that are believed to be home to mysterious creatures are glacial in nature—bodies of water that became isolated from the ocean eons ago and trapped ancient lifeforms that have either gone extinct in the broader world or are hidden in depths that prevent us from finding them. The lake, in this theory, either serves as a protective habitat that prevents the species from becoming extinct or simply provides fewer opportunities to hide and allows them to be seen more often.

It wouldn't be unfair, then, to assume that the D/FW area lakes are devoid of such exciting sightings since Texas lacks glacial lakes or ancient trapped oceans. In truth, the D/FW Metroplex lacks natural lakes entirely. All large bodies of water are the result of impounding the Trinity River and its tributaries. The oldest of these man-made lakes is White Rock Lake (White Rock Dam was built in 1911), and most were created in the '50s and '60s. But despite the young age of the metroplex's lakes, its waterways aren't free from enigmatic critters.

Beyond giant man-eating catfish lurking in the lakes (don't worry, we'll talk about them shortly), most D/FW residents would be at a loss if forced to name a singular lake monster native to the region, which is a bit sad considering there is only one. But yes, the North Texas region does have an aquatic cryptid that, in many ways, is not only as intriguing as its more famous Scottish cousin but also might even be related to it.

Fun party trivia: In 1947, there was a Lake Worth Monster that made national news and became a bit of a fascination, until Thurman Leroy

Rench, the marina manager, admitted to the hoax. It seems he intended it to only scare off several women who would fish there daily and block boats from docking. He would drag a damaged and deflated inner tube across the water with a wench. Mr. Rench claimed to have sewn two green buttons on it for eyes, which, when combined with the wench, was sufficient to terrorize his elderly agitators. The name given to this vicious-looking inner tube would be reused twenty years later when John Reichart had his run-in with a particularly persnickety Sasquatch.

Ol' One Eye

Lake Granbury's Monster

After midnight one day in May 2019, Robert King and a friend of his were enjoying an evening of night fishing when Mr. King snagged a "big one" (bigger than he suspected). At first, he thought that perhaps he'd gotten tangled on a submerged tree branch when the line moved, indicating something living had taken his bait and was hooked. He fought for over an hour, even moving the boat closer to their target, and when they realized that the "fish" was near the surface, Robert's friend shone their light into the water to get a look at what Mr. King had caught. But instead of seeing a large grass carp or channel catfish, they saw an eye.

"It was dark, so all I could see was the eye, but it was big.... [The eye was] about two to two and a half inches across." Robert noted, "The weird thing is that it didn't look like a fish eye. It was like a person's eye. It was round like a fish, but it had a white around the iris like a person." Possibly scared by the light, the creature, according to Mr. King, "rolled over and swam away with my new $300 fishing pole!"

While no fish known to live in the lake are large enough to match Mr. King's description, there are accounts of an unknown animal seen in Lake Granbury's waters that might explain Mr. King's encounter: Ol' One Eye. Though it is not seen often, in many ways, the description of Lake Granbury's resident monster is fairly common. While it is unclear where the creature's moniker came from, Ol' One Eye appears to be a long, dark gray serpentine creature with a humped back like Nessie (the Loch Ness Monster) and Champy (the Lake Champlain Monster). Initially this would lead one to interpret the anomalous animal to be a plesiosaur-esque creature like the

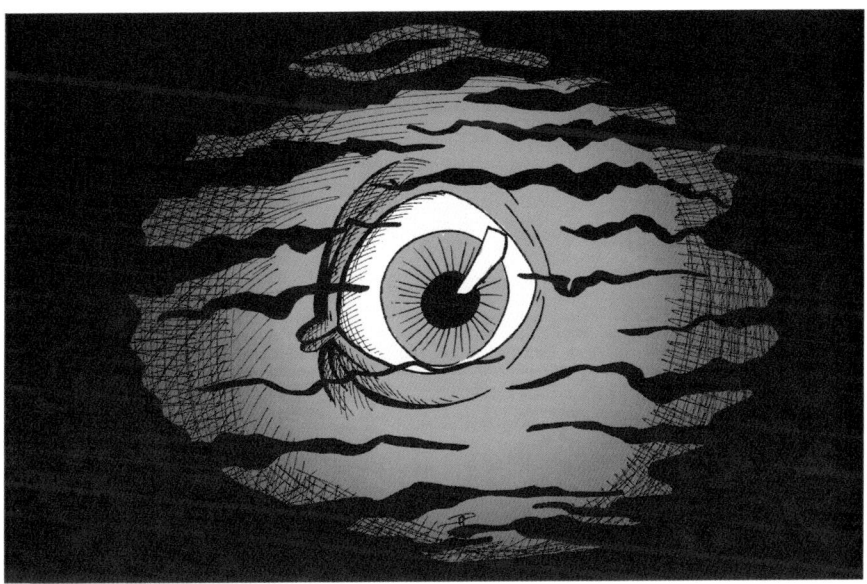

Depiction of the creature's eye seen by Mr. King and his friend. *Illustration by the author.*

ones described in Lake Ogopogo, Loch Ness or Lake Champlain, but this is not the case. The best description of the mysterious inhabitant comes from an account recorded by famed researchers Nick Redfern and Shelly Covington-Montana.

It was a hot August Saturday afternoon (for those unfamiliar with the area, there is no such thing as a "cool" August day—only days that aren't as blisteringly hot as others) in 1999, when a woman we'll call Tanya saw something incredible. She was walking along Lake Granbury's picturesque banks, when suddenly, a large eel-shaped creature violently rocketed out of Lake Granbury and temporarily beached itself. This strange creature whipped around on the shore for fifteen to twenty seconds before returning to the refuge of the water. Since the animal was mostly exposed and using its entire body to dislodge itself, Tanya could actually see One Eye in its entirety.

According to Tanya, One Eye was a seventeen-foot-long, two-foot-wide eel. She didn't mention how many eyes it had. According to Mr. Redfern, Tanya "was in no doubt whatsoever that it was a gigantic eel." It should be noted that the American eel (*Anguilla rostrate*) is native to Texas rivers and was quite common until the construction of dams ended its northward migrations, which has, according to the Texas Parks and Wildlife Department, "eliminated this species from most central and western

Ol' One Eye himself. *Illustration by the author.*

Rendering of large *Atractosteus spatula*, also known as alligator gar. *Illustration by the author.*

areas of the state." Given this information and the fact that the largest American eel on record is just less than five feet long, a native eel species does seem an unlikely option. However, the aforementioned researcher Shelly Covington-Montana does have a native Texan as a potential suspect for Ol' One Eye: *Atractosteus spatula*.

More commonly known as the alligator gar, *Atractosteus spatula* has an odd morphology (particularly in extreme sizes) that could lead someone unfamiliar with the species to mistake it for an eel. Though the average mature alligator gar is between six and eight feet long, there are numerous anecdotal accounts of the vicious-looking lepisosteiformes growing beyond ten feet. A perfect example comes from the childhood of Shelly's husband, Don Covington. While fishing with his father in their fourteen-foot-long bass boat, Don snagged what they immediately knew was an extremely large gar. While they were trying to land the enormous fish (and before the line broke), Don and his father realized that the creature was longer than the boat they were in. Though unconfirmed, Don's story has a great deal of company around Texas and should not be ignored.

Adding more credibility to Robert's story is Shelly's observation that the eye on a gar can appear similar to a dolphin's when you pull the fish out of the water. When removed from the water, the membrane surrounding the gar's eye can appear white, giving it a more human appearance. While it is true that Robert never pulled his felonious fish out of the water, it could be that the same phenomenon noted by Mrs. Covington-Montana occurs for a fish of such an unusual size close to the surface of the lake.

"It's not just the eye itself," Mrs. Covington-Montana noted. "It's the placement of the eye and the surrounding area; it just doesn't look like the typical fish eye of say a bass or crappie. Additionally, predators' eyes are more forward facing, while prey is outward facing. Given this, the eye of a super-sized gar may appear less like a fish and more like a creature." And while an alligator gar of enormous proportions is a likely culprit, there is still the question of Ol' One Eye's purported gray coloring and humped back, which is distinctly different from that of any known gar, regardless of size.

So, does this mean Ol' One Eye is an ancient surviving plesiosaur or some other aquatic animal believed to have gone extinct in deep antiquity, like the Loch Ness Monster? As noted earlier, the problem of Lake Granbury trapping and isolating something exotic is that while Loch Ness and other ancient glacial lakes were cut off from the ocean thousands of years ago, Lake Granbury was only created in 1969. But this fact doesn't necessarily preclude Ol' One Eye from being something exotic—or even related to the Loch Ness Monster.

Nick Redfern noted, "Although the lake itself is less than half a century old, the Brazos River [the river that was impounded to create Lake Granbury] has a long history of sightings of huge fish and mysterious creatures. Native Americans and early Spaniards talked of something terrible and savage lurking in the river."

There is a story as old as the state of Texas itself, at least according to Word War II veteran and Texas native Andrew Garrett, of a young American

Indian child gathering water from the Brazos. There was a deer that also stopped to drink from the river on the opposite side. While he was looking at the deer, a giant serpent reached out of the water and snatched it to make a meal of the poor creature. The child dropped his buckets and ran down the river, away from the monster's head. After running for two miles, he realized he'd reached the snake's tail. While clearly an exaggerated tale (pun intended), it serves as confirmation of Mr. Redfern's assertion that the Brazos River has a long history of monstrous sea serpents navigating its waters, and one or more of these animals could have become trapped in the lake.

The term "sea serpent" may seem an incorrect designation, as the Brazos is a freshwater river, but it might be more applicable than one would assume. The Brazos does empty into the Gulf of Mexico, and many fish species either live in the ocean and swim into fresh water to spawn or, as in the case of the American eel, spawn in the ocean and then live in freshwater rivers and lakes. This opens up the possibility of Ol' One Eye not necessarily being a resident of Lake Granbury but instead a visitor.

The size of the creature and recent nature of the sightings supports this concept. Some fish species can live for unusually long times—centuries even—and it is of note that the longfin eel of Australia and New Zealand has an average lifespan of around sixty years, and some have even been found to live over one hundred years. That last part is of importance because Tanya did say that the seventeen-foot-long creature she saw in 1999 reminded her of a giant eel. Moreover, the eye of the European conger eel does have a white area around the iris, in the same way Robert King described. Additionally, the European conger eel is not only gray but can also grow over twenty feet in length.

While the possibility of a giant European conger eel does seem a bit out of the running, as congers are native to the Mediterranean and the Atlantic, it must be noted that many species of ocean-going fish can move into fresh water (bull sharks being the most famous). It is entirely possible that a rogue conger was able to adapt to the Brazos's fresh water and then found itself trapped in Lake Granbury after the dam was erected, as many have suggested is the case for the Loch Ness Monster.

It was announced in the fall of 2019 that the results of a massive environmental eDNA metabarcoding survey performed on Loch Ness provided no novel or unknown species currently residing in the famed lake. eDNA metabarcoding is a relatively new technology that allows scientists to collect water from different locations and depths and pull the DNA from the random particulate material sluffed off by the resident fauna and then

Drawing of a European conger eel. *Illustration by the author.*

catalogue it. Giant invasive catfish and Greenland sharks had been proposed as possible identities for Nessie, but no catfish or shark DNA was discovered. That being said, they did find eel DNA—lots of it.

Obviously, finding eel DNA doesn't come as a surprise, given the abundance of eels living in Loch Ness at all depths, but it does lend credence to the idea that Nessie is a supersized eel. It is entirely possible that if a small population of European conger eel (or even a single individual) were responsible for the Nessie sightings, then the DNA obtained from the samples was degraded sufficiently to make it indistinguishable from the local freshwater eels native to the loch. However, neither the Loch Ness Monster nor Ol' One Eye need be a wayward conger to be an eel.

Professor Neil J. Gemmell, the gentleman who headed up the Loch Ness genomic survey, was kind enough to answer several of my questions and confirm a few things. While the lack of European conger eel DNA doesn't necessarily close the door on the possibility of a wayward oceanic eel, it does give credence to an even more interesting possibility: an unrecognized mutation of the native European eel (*Anguilla anguilla*). Since the survey was designed to look for the species (a remarkable achievement really), it wouldn't detect a subtle genetic mutation allowing for substantial growth.

Professor Gemmell noted, "Our study tells us nothing about size. There may be unusually large common eels in Loch Ness—lots of anecdotal evidence, but no pictures, no recorded catches." Additionally, because the line between species and subspecies can be blurry, the good professor did indicate that if there was an unrecognized giant subspecies of the native freshwater eels, they wouldn't necessarily show as distinct from the larger *Anguilla anguilla* population.

So, if the most famous lake monster in the world has a real possibility of being either an enlarged freshwater eel or a giant conger visiting its cousins, then Ol' One Eye also has a possibility of being the same thing—a massive eel as Tanya claimed. Just because *Anguilla rostrate* (the American eel) was the only officially recognized freshwater eel native to North America, that doesn't mean there isn't a conger that prefers freshwater lakes and found itself trapped when the Brazos River was dammed. Or there could be a completely unknown subspecies of the American eel that shares several coloration and morphological similarities to the European conger chilling out in the picturesque reservoir.

The Trinity River Titan

Just so that everyone is on the same page, at 710 miles long, the Trinity is the longest river in Texas to have a watershed entirely within the state. While the bulk of the river is one continuous stream south of Dallas that eventually empties into the Texas Gulf at Galveston Bay, the Trinity has four branches (Clear Fork, West Fork, Elm Fork and the East Fork) that spread out across North Texas. The Trinity River and its many tributaries made long-term human settlements possible in the region for as long as humans have been in Texas.

Robert Cavelier de La Salle initially called the Trinity the "River of Canoes" because it was used for trade by the indigenous populations and then the European settlers. Until the arrival of trains to Dallas, the Trinity River was essential for transporting goods to market on steamships and flat-bottom boats. For the last one hundred years or so, the Trinity has had several branches dammed to create reservoirs for water to support North Texas's growing population, with the main river being used largely for

The Trinity Titan. *Illustration by the author.*

recreation—fishing in particular. Given the Trinity's popularity for sport fishing, it isn't any surprise that researcher Tim Henderson's older brother would be found there, near Crockett, Texas, on a particularly interesting day in 1979.

Around twenty-seven at the time, Tim's brother had an encounter that would impact his life, and the life of his brother, forever. What follows is an account of the elder Mr. Henderson's sighting as recorded by his brother Tim:

> *I was just fishing on the little peninsula, like I always did because it was a good spot for bass. The water was about five feet down from the edge of the bank of where I was standing. The water was calm and slow moving. I never knew how deep the water may have been there. All of a sudden, there was a very large swirl in the water and up came a creature I was not prepared to lay my eyes on. It rose completely straight out of the water to a height of about ten feet. It was even with the top of my head. I saw its left side. It was completely black, and the width of the body was larger in diameter than a fifty-five-gallon oil barrel* [about two feet].

> *The eye was as large as the diameter of a coffee cup saucer. The mouth it had was approximately four feet long, with many sharp pointed teeth, like that of a pike or gar and were at least four inches in length. It had very large scales. It was as black as coal. It looked exactly like what is depicted as an ichthyosaurus that you see in museums and books. I never saw a fin or any other appendage it may have had, as they must have been down below the surface. I just stood there, frozen in shock, until I realized it was looking directly at me. It was only about eight feet away and could have easily reached over to grab me up, like I was an easy picking for a meal and that I was on the menu.*
>
> *I just started slowly backing up, away from the edge of the little peninsula, toward my truck. After some paces back, making distance between the creature and I, it just slipped straight down back into the water. I got out of there and never went back to that spot again. I did not know things could get that big in fresh water. I will never forget how it looked or how it was staring right at me.*

Tim and his brother have discussed this encounter for decades, and at no point has his brother ever entertained the idea that what he saw was an alligator gar of unusual size. "He's absolutely certain of what he saw, and the only thing he's ever said got close to it are drawings of ichthyosaurs he's found in books and encyclopedias." As an avid fisherman and outdoorsman, the witness's familiarity with the local fauna should be taken seriously. Given that Don Covington's account, and other accounts of giant alligator gar found among the anglers of the D/FW region, indicates that the monster gar are easily distinguished as being nothing more than exceptionally large gar, it must be concluded that this creature isn't a gar but something else entirely.

Given the similarity (of coloration at least) between Ol' One Eye and this creature, as well as the fact that, like the Brazos, the Trinity River empties into the Gulf of Mexico (separated by only about fifty miles or so), the Titan could potentially be the same kind of creature found in Lake Granbury. Even the fact that the Titan stuck its head out is reminiscent of a moray eel sticking its head out of a hole and could be seen as evidence for this theory. However, Mr. Henderson noted that the creature he saw had very large scales, which is uncommon for large ocean-going eel species. While the presence of scales does fall in the not-a-giant-eel category, certain freshwater eels do have scales. Additionally, there are "armored" catfish, so the idea that a giant undiscovered species of eel could have scales or armor that could be seen as scales is not out of the picture.

Even the morphology of the creature's head and face doesn't take eels out of the running. While this couldn't be a stray European conger, there are eel species with more elongated and slender faces. The three known species of snipe eels have exceptionally long and narrow faces, so an unknown species of eel that can survive in fresh water and grow to enormous size is still a possibility. However, Mr. Henderson's account does specifically note that he didn't see any fins, and an eel's fins would have been noticeable, as the head was so far out of the water.

The mass of the head described was significant, and to be lifted more than four feet above the waterline requires significant leverage, indicating the creature was either absolutely massive or that it had appendages (legs or flippers) that were supporting and lifting out of the Trinity's water. It is important to point out that we do depict ichthyosaurs with flippers, which would allow this creature to rise up. Obviously, Mr. Henderson didn't see enough of the creature to make a definite identification, but he didn't see the dolphin-like dorsal fin that is common among the ichthyosauria.

Reconstruction of Clidastes Pro Python. *Illustration by the author.*

Given that most basal ichthyosaurs, like Chaohusaurus, were too small to be what Mr. Henderson saw, it doesn't rule out a new species that is currently unknown. But it does lead one to look at the clidastes group from the mosasaur family. Like the ichthyosaurs, the mosasaurs were marine reptiles similar to the monitor lizards, like the Komodo dragon.

While stories of mosasaur-like creatures have surfaced in the Mediterranean and Atlantic, support for the idea that the Trinity Titan was a relic marine reptile comes from a publication known as *The World of Wonders*, published in the late 1870s. It was the report of a Captain A. Hassel of a ship called the *St. Olaf* that was sailing in the Gulf of Mexico. His ship was two days out from Galveston when he and the crew saw what they described as a seventy-foot-long serpent that was six feet in diameter and had three fins on its back. Captain Hassel's creature was yellow, and the head was not mentioned as being anything too dissimilar from a snake's, so we can presume this is not Mr. Henderson's Trinity Titan. But the existence of this unknown creature in the Gulf of Mexico opens up the possibilities for the Titan (and Ol' One Eye for that matter) to be something far more exotic than an undiscovered species of eel.

Interestingly, the image included is of a member of the clidastes group of mosasaurinae, and the smallest of the clidastes was the *Dallasaurus turneri*, which was discovered in Cedar Hill by amateur fossil hunter Van Turner.

Giant Catfish

While most North Texas anglers have a personal story or know someone who has a personal story of a giant alligator gar, *everyone* in the D/FW Metroplex knows about the giant catfish that lurk beneath the dark waters of the area's reservoirs. It has been mentioned but does bear repeating that nearly every large lake (even most ponds) aren't naturally occurring but instead were made by damming up sections of the Trinity and Brazos Rivers, their tributaries or forks. While a maximum depth of forty to seventy-five feet doesn't seem like that much of a change, it should be noted (according to the University of Illinois at Urbana-Champaign Department of Physics) that the pressure exerted by water increases by 0.433 psi (pounds per square inch) for every foot you descend. (Sea water weighs 0.445 psi.)

For those unfamiliar with this principle, at sea level, the earth's atmosphere is pushing down on you at a weight of 14.7 psi, and your body is designed to operate in this particular condition. This is why when you fly in an airplane or drive up a mountain, your ears pop when you reach a particular altitude. The reduction in atmospheric pressure creates a difference with the pressures in your inner ears, and your body has to equalize it. The same thing happens when you scuba dive or even go to the bottom of a swimming pool deeper than 10.0 feet. The deeper you travel under water, the more the pressure increases. At a mere depth of 33.95 feet, you actually double the psi found at the lake's surface, and at 68.0 feet, you have tripled the pressure. The pressures found in these impounded rivers have created new environments for native species that were adapted to living in shallow rivers and creeks, and according to some divers, no fish has taken advantage of this change more than some catfish.

According to researcher and dive enthusiast Tex, the giant catfish urban legends are more than just legends:

> *I had the opportunity to go on a night dive at Possum Kingdom Lake, and I jumped at it because I'd never gone on one...and we were swimming with a seven-foot line between myself and the instructor for safety. Well, during the dive, a giant catfish comes out of nowhere and literally slaps me in the face with the biggest tail fan I've ever seen and swam off. I learn later that while I'm getting fish slapped, the head of this catfish is up with my instructor, so this thing had to be around at least seven feet long.*

Since Texas catfish shouldn't be getting bigger than sixty inches (five feet), the presence of a seven-footer confirmed the validity of the stories Tex had heard from the maintenance divers who work on the dam at Possum Kingdom Lake (also created by impounding water from the Brazos River). Apparently, it was common for divers to bring broom handles and other batons to help them move giant catfish out of their way to work on the dam at certain depths. "The fish are so big down there you can ride them, but they're so big that they don't really want to move. So, they just float there at the bottom near the dam eating all the dead fish and trash. So, the maintenance guys just poke them and encourage them to move over a bit, and they do."

While Tex's informants are confirming the story that every North Texan has grown up hearing, it does bear noting that, according to the Texas Parks and Wildlife Department (TPWD), the largest catfish of any species caught in Texas was a 121.5-pound *Ictalurus furcatus*. The blue catfish, the largest of the catfish species native to North America, was caught on January 16, 2004, by Cody Mullennix at Lake Texoma. Texoma was formed by impounding water from the Red River, which serves as the border between Texas and Oklahoma, hence "Tex" for Texas and "Oma" for Oklahoma. (Cedar Hill was named because it had a hill covered in cedar trees, and Round Rock was named after a big circular-shaped rock. Nobody ever said Texans were known for naming things creatively.)

At first, the discrepancy between the official record catch and the purported size of the monster catfish would seem to file the creatures safely in the big-fish-story category, but most of the tackle used by freshwater anglers could never land a five-hundred- or six-hundred-pound catfish. Forget the strength any fish that size would have; the weight of it alone would cause any line used to snap—not to mention that the depth these things have been found (Possum Kingdom is around one hundred feet deep) is well below what most people would fish. So, it isn't really surprising that these monsters haven't been caught, or at least reeled in. "I wouldn't be surprised if people have caught these things in the past," Tex noted, "but they're just so big that they break the line or steal the pole and swim away."

Assuming that Tex's observations and the accounts of numerous divers are accurate, it is worth asking if any species of catfish could naturally grow to the sizes mentioned and make actual capture nearly impossible for an unprepared angler. Yes, they can. The Mekong giant catfish is currently the largest catfish on record, with the official record being 8.9 feet long and weighing in at 669 pounds. The wels catfish is known to be similar sizes, and several credible accounts from the nineteenth century indicate that 9.8-foot-long, 550-pound specimen had been caught. It is believed that the wels can top 16.0 feet in length and weigh over 660 pounds. So, in general, it is within the realm of possibility that a giant catfish exists—at least theoretically—but would a bottom-feeder like a catfish ever attack a human? Again, yes.

Bagarius yarelli, also known as goonch, are giant catfish found in India's Kali River that are known to grow to 6.5 feet in length and weigh over two hundred pounds. Oh, and they have been known to attack and kill both humans and large livestock. The accounts of goonch killing and consuming humans are more than mere folklore—the attacks have been cataloged and are considered credible by the local authorities. Perhaps the most disturbing discovery concerning these attacks was uncovered by several researchers who investigated the claims in the early 2000s. The researchers determined that if the goonch is actually the culprit, the catfish in question would only need to weigh between two hundred and three hundred pounds, with a length of 6.0 feet to succeed in its assault on a full-grown man.

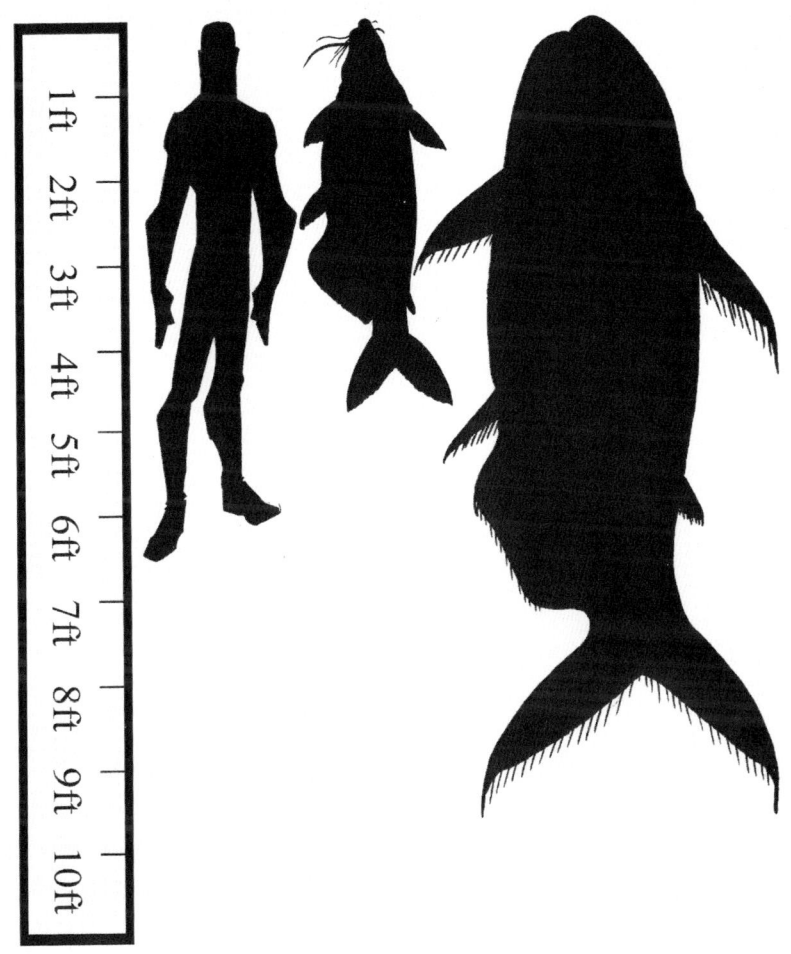

Comparison chart of the largest catfish caught in Texas waters and the world's largest catfish, caught in the Mekong delta. *Illustration by the author.*

So, yes, giant man-eating catfish do exist, but do they exist in Texas waterways? While there have been examples of changes in environment causing sudden changes in the physiology of certain fish, it is worth asking whether the increase in water pressure, reduction of temperature and abundance of food really explain the alleged massive increase in size. Since the goonch, wels and other worldwide species have been able to grow to their monumental sizes in shallower waters and with less opportunity than the average blue catfish, we should consider other options as well.

Given the ease with which invasive exotic fish like freshwater stingrays, paku (an omnivorous relative of the piranha) and others have set up large populations in Texas lakes and rivers, we should ask if these mysterious siluriformes are actually a native species. Aside from the possibility of the fish being brought over as pets and then released once they grew too large for their tanks, they could have been shipped live to be sold as food, only to find themselves in a creek or lake instead of being disposed of properly. (According to the TPWD, both happen all the time.)

Whether these giant whiskered devils are a native species that are adapting to the change in the environment or an invasive exotic species appears irrelevant. From anecdotal evidence to recorded events and specimens, it certainly seems that the possibility of these beasts being large enough to view humans as foodstuff should be taken seriously. That being said, according to Tex, these peculiar pangasiidae were not active predators. While they appear threatening, they are lazy and sluggish creatures—a far cry from the man-eating marine monsters North Texans warn their children about.

Fun party trivia: The round rock for which Round Rock, Texas, was named was a large circular stone found at a particularly shallow section of Brushy Creek used as a crossing on the famous Chisholm Trail. If the stone could be seen, then it was safe to cross, and if the waters covered it, then those traveling knew to not chance it. So many wagons crossed at the round rock that the worn impressions of the wagon wheel tracks can still be seen.

Conclusion

Next time you get a chance to visit the D/FW region, I suggest that once you've enjoyed all of the attractions, museums and restaurants, take an opportunity to visit some of the smaller towns mentioned in this book and take the backroads to get there. Go fishing in one of the lakes or explore some of the many nature trails. D/FW's large prairies and white stone creeks are worth more than a passing glance, particularly in the spring when the bluebonnets and Indian paintbrushes are in bloom.

After all, you never know what you might find.

—JGM

Bibliography

Alan. "Dr. Kent Hovind—Pterodactyl Sighting Interview." August 12, 2019. Youtube.com.
Butler, Steven. "Legend Hold That a Specter Known as 'The Lady of the Lake' Haunts White Rock Lake Park." Scenic White Rock Lake Park. 1996. http://www.watermelon-kid.com.
Carrol, Jeff. "Sublime, TX." Texas Historical Association. June 15, 2010. https://tshaonline.org.
Cedar Hill Book Project. *History of Cedar Hill, Texas*. Wolfe City, TX: Henington Publishing Company, 2002.
Clarke, Sallie Ann. *The Lake Worth Monster of Greer Island, Ft. Worth, Texas*. Fort Worth, TX: Self-Published, 1969.
Colvard, Matthew, interview with author. September 20, 2019.
Connors, Deborah T., and S. Alan Skinner. *Archaeological Investigations at Lakeview Lake*. Dallas, TX: Archaeology Research Program Southern Methodist University, 1979.
Covington-Montana, Shelly, interview with author. September 30, 2019.
Creeker. "Hauntings Ghosts and Monsters of Ellis County." *Ellis County Texas History* (blog). October 27, 2007. http://blogforelliscountytexashistory.blogspot.com.
Dallas Historical Society. http://www.dallashistory.org.
Daniels, Christine, and Rose Daniels, interview with author. August 20, 2019.
Dillon, David. "Time and a River: A Journey along Legendary White Rock Creek from Prehistory to the Present." *D Magazine*, October 1979.
Elam, Richard. "Johnson County." Texas State Historical Association. January 28, 2012. https://tshaonline.org.

BIBLIOGRAPHY

Gard, Wayne. "Trinity River." Texas State Historical Association. June 30, 2010. https://tshaonline.org.

Garrett, Andrew, interview with author. July 12, 1995.

Gemmell, Professor Neil J., interview with author. December 1, 2019.

George, Andrew. *The Epic of Gilgamesh*. London: Penguin Classic, 2003.

Gerhard, Ken, interview with author. October 2, 2019.

Glasscock, Todd. "Old Foamy Road Monster Still Just a Legend." *Cleburne Times-Review*, October 28, 2016. https://www.cleburnetimesreview.com.

Gonzalez, Jon. "Monster of Cedar Hill." *True Horror Stories of Texas* (blog). February 28, 2019. https://truehorrorstoriesoftexas.com.

———, email interview with author. December 17, 2019.

Greene, Angie, interview with author. June 16, 2019.

Haaser, Robert J. "Italy, TX." Texas State Historical Association. June 15, 2010. https://tshaonline.org.

Hardy, Heck, Moore Cultural Resource Consultants. "Ellis County History Overview." Ancestory. September 6, 2002. http://sites.rootsweb.com.

Henderson, Tim, interview with author. August 21, 2019.

Jasinski, Laurie E. "Avalon, TX (Ellis County)." Texas State Historical Association. June 9, 2010. https://tshaonline.org.

King, Robert, interview with author. August 12, 2019.

Knollman, April, interview with author. March 5, 2015.

Kolbsterjr. "Old Foamy, a Legend? I Think Not!" Reddit. November 13, 2012. https://www.reddit.com.

Machann, Clinton. "Czechs." Texas State Historical Association. June 12, 2010. https://tshaonline.org.

Marines, Claudia, interview with author. August 5, 2019.

Masterson, W.R. "Luke Short—A Dandy Gyunfighter." *Human Life Magazine*, 1907.

Mentz, Daniel, interview with author. December 16, 2018.

Mijares, Rachel, interview with author. November 2, 2019.

Montgomery, Murray. "Wild Woman of the Navidad." Texas Escapes. September 13, 2005. http://www.texasescapes.com.

"Occupational Employment Statistics." U.S. Census Bureau. October 8, 2019. *https://www.bls.gov*.

Odom, E. Dale. "Denton County." Texas State Hitorical Association. June 12, 2010. https://tshaonline.org.

Orozco, Sara, interview with author. August 5, 2019.

Perez, Angelica, interview with author. August 5, 2019.

Perez, Raymond, interview with author. June 15, 2014.

Redfern, Nick. "Bridging the World of the Supernatural." Mysterious Universe. May 17, 2019. https://mysteriousuniverse.org.

Bibliography

———. "Creature of the Month: One Eye." *Nick Redfern's World of Whatever* (blog). July 31, 2017. http://nickredfernfortean.blogspot.com.

———. "Goat Man Haunts the Bridge." Mysterious Universe. June 18, 2013. https://mysteriousuniverse.org.

———. "Goat-Man Panic in the Lone Star State." Mysterious Universe. November 14, 2017. https://mysteriousuniverse.org.

———, interview with author. September 20, 2019.

———. *Memoirs of a Monster Hunter: A Five-Year Journey in Search of the Unknown.* Franklin Lakes, NJ: New Page Books, 2007.

———. "The Men in Black: Tulpas?" Mysterious Universe. February 15, 2019. https://mysteriousuniverse.org.

Schmelzer, Janet. "Forth Worth, TX." Texas State Historical Association. June 12, 2010. https://tshaonline.org.

Smith, Leondre, interview with author. June 17, 2017.

Stewart, Jeff, interview with author. July 22, 2019.

Stowers, Carlton. "Cedar Hill, TX (Dallas County)." Texas State Historical Association. June 12, 2010. https://tshaonline.org.

Stringer, Dr. Tommy. "Stringer—How Did Dallas Get Its Name?" *Corsicana Daily Sun*, April 12, 2008.

Taylor, Joe, interview with author. January 6, 2018.

Tentzer, Pastor Bruce. http://www.trinityrivercorridor.org/html/great_trinity_forest.html. December 1, 2019.

Tex, interview with author. November 15, 2019.

Trinity River Corridor Project. http://www.trinityrivercorridor.org.

Urban, Rachel, interview with author. February 18, 2018.

Wade, Harry E. "Peters Colony." Texas State Historical Association. June 15, 2010. https://tshaonline.org.

"Wandering Shaman 'Mistaken' for Bigfoot in North Carolina." BBC News, August 10, 2017. https://www.bbc.com.

Weiser, Kathy. "Alton, Texas and the Haunted Goatman's Bridge." Legends of America. November 15, 2010. https://www.legendsofamerica.com.

West, Martin Litchfield. *Indo-European Poetry and Myth.* Oxford, UK: Oxford University Press, 2007.

Wolff, H.N. "Gilgamesh, Enkidu, and the Heroic Life." *Journal of the American Oriental Society* (1969): 392–98.

Wooster, Robert. "U.S. Army on the Texas Frontier." Texas Beyond History. June 30, 2003. https://texasbeyondhistory.net.

Xerxes, R. John. "1836, Nacogdoches, Texas: Davy Crockett and the Bigfoot's Prophecy." *Today in Bigfood History* (blog). May 15, 2012. https://bigfoothistory.wordpress.com.

About the Author

Author and founder of the Society for the Investigation and Research of the Unknown (SIRU), Jason McLean was born and raised in DeSoto, Texas. He currently lives in Waxahachie with his wife and children, via Nacogdoches, Texas, where he and his wife graduated from Stephen F. Austin University. When not appearing on several weekly vodcasts or traveling North Texas for business, Jason can be found at his art desk in the back half of the closet he claimed much to the chagrin of his long-suffering wife's wardrobe.